D0278167

◆ PRIMARY SCHOOLS AND THE FUTURE

PRIMARY SCHOOLS AND THE FUTURE

Celebration, challenges and choices

Patrick Whitaker

Open University Press
Buckingham • Philadelphia

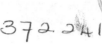

Open University Press
Celtic Court
22 Ballmoor
Buckingham
MK18 1XW

and
1900 Frost Road, Suite 101
Bristol, PA 19007, USA

First Published 1997

A catalogue record of this book is available from the British Library

ISBN   0 335 19423 0 (pb)   0 335 19424 9 (hb)

Library of Congress Cataloging-in-Publication Data
Whitaker, Patrick.
    Primary schools and the future: celebration, challenges, and
choices / Patrick Whitaker.
        p. cm.
    Includes bibliographical references and index.
    ISBN 0–335–19424–9 (hb). — ISBN 0–335–19423–0 (pb)
    1. Education, Elementary—Great Britain. 2. Elementary schools—
Great Britain. I. Title.
LA633. W45 1997
372.941—dc20
                                                                96–24014
                                                                CIP

Typeset by Graphicraft Typesetters Ltd, Hong Kong
Printed in Great Britain by Biddles Ltd, Guildford and King's Lynn

To all lovers of primary schools, and those who work in them.

 CONTENTS

Preface   viii

1   THE CHANGING WORLD   1

2   THE PARADIGM SHIFT   18

3   ACHIEVEMENT AND POTENTIAL   34

4   LEARNING AND TEACHING   51

5   CULTURE AND WELL-BEING   68

6   GETTING THINGS DONE   87

7   TEAMWORK AND COLLABORATION   108

8   TRANSFORMATIVE LEADERSHIP   127

9   MEETING THE FUTURE   143

10 NEW MILLENNIUM EDUCATORS   162

Bibliography   169
Index   172

 # PREFACE

The idea for this book had been growing in my mind for some time, but only became clear while I was watching a television programme in which Sir John Harvey Jones was conducting one of his troubleshooter projects. The film showed him in a rather delapidated industrial building. He looked round, shook his head reflectively and then partly to his host and partly to himself said, 'I just love factories'. It was the power and utter simplicity of this statement which struck me. I knew exactly what he meant, because it was then that I realized that for the whole of my professional life I had loved primary schools, and that is what I wanted to write about. The book has provided a rich opportunity for me to examine the nature of this passion, to tease out its many facets and to uncover some of its fine details.

This book is also prompted by a sadness that our primary schools have become so unfairly ridiculed. The vast majority of parents, I believe, appreciate the enormous contribution our primary schools make to their communities, and to society as a whole. Many know that if their children are happy at school, it is because they are taught effectively and well managed. The primary school tradition in this country is an honourable and innovative one. Primary school teachers, past and present, have made significant contributions to society; sadly, such contributions are today insufficiently acknowledged and celebrated.

The book has two main purposes. The first is to consider the challenges facing primary schools as they move towards a new century and a new millennium. It proposes that the times we are in, with their mounting pressures and increasing tensions, have the characteristics of an evolutionary crisis, in which the knowledge and the traditions of the past no longer seem to serve our own best interests. Fast and accelerating change in the world has left many of us bewildered and perplexed, feeling that our capacities to manage effectively are being tested beyond their perceived capacities. We seem to be in a constant state of turbulence as we struggle to respond to relentless change, mounting pressure and increasing inconsistency. We feel confused that the world we have inherited is not the same as the one that our upbringing and education were supposed to have prepared us for.

The lessons from evolutionary theory are stark and clear. If we carry on as usual, in one way or another we will not make it. Everything depends upon our capacity to adapt, to discover new ways of managing the novel circumstances emerging all around us. We need to learn faster than we have in the past, and to be prepared to jettison some cherished ideas and strong beliefs. These new challenges present serious choices about what we should do, and what directions we should take. The maps into the future are sketchy and there is much exploring to be done. For those charged with plotting the new pathways and future direction of primary school education, the challenge is both daunting and exciting.

The second purpose of the book is to celebrate the work of primary schools and to note their unique qualities and achievements. Contrary to general perception, primary schools are not simple organizations with a straightforward task. They are as complex as any organization in society, with tasks as difficult to manage as those asked of any profession. My current professional work regularly brings me into contact with primary school teachers, who are experiencing the deep pain of a profession whose integrity is held in question, whose commitment is treated with contempt and whose work is commented on with scorn. But despite all this, they display a resilient commitment to their task and a huge ambition for the pupils in their care. Most have experienced a deep encroachment of professional activity into their personal and social lives and mounting expectations of their role in curing society of its discomforts and insecurities.

Within these two broad purposes are four specific aims:

1 To examine the changed and changing circumstances within which primary school education is now set.
2 To explore the unique organizational features of primary schools and their potential for dynamic development.
3 To outline specific strategies to meet the challenges of the future.
4 To consider the nature of the educational leadership that will be required.

The book could not have been written without the cooperation of all those primary school headteachers, deputy heads, curriculum coordinators and classroom teachers I have worked with over recent years. This book is both for them, and about them, and I hope it reveals my deep respect and admiration for what they do. I am also grateful to all those local education authorities who have offered me so many interesting opportunities to work with their primary school teachers, and to the many universities who have invited me to share in their professional development work. Finally, my thanks to the publishers, Open University Press, not only because they continue to give me so many opportunities to write, but because they, too, are an organization with a foot firmly in the next century.

Patrick Whitaker

◆ 1 ▶ THE CHANGING WORLD

In primary schools over the past decade, we have witnessed an increasing sense of frustration about the management of education. Teachers have absorbed an enormous range of changes to an already complex system, but have also experienced the society they serve appearing to turn on them, blaming them for all the current ills and difficulties of the nation. Schools seem to have become the scapegoat of a society ill at ease with itself, and confused about which direction it needs to take into the future.

As we approach the millennium, it is useful to place current experience in the wider context of change and development, and this chapter highlights some of the less visible but deeply felt factors which are affecting our lives, creating a crisis in organizational confidence, as well as in self-belief and well-being. While we know that things are not like they used to be, we are not always clear why. Neither are we sure what we have to do to overcome our present difficulties. The future is unclear, prediction is hazardous and for many there seems little hope. As we become more aware of the dynamics of this evolutionary crisis, we will be in a better position to plan the adaptations required to survive the pressures that bear down and threaten us.

In our journey into the future, primary schools will have a vital part to play in this process of evolution and adaptation. The success of future adults to ride with confidence the waves of continuous change they will undoubtedly experience, will depend to a greater extent than in the past on the nature and quality of their earliest experiences in the schooling system. Our primary schools are a vital key to the future.

CHANGING LIVES, CHANGING TIMES

In these days of personal pressure and social hyperactivity, the future has a habit of arriving before we are really ready for it. This creates an inexorable sense of crisis management in which somewhat haphazard events and incidents seem to run our lives, rather than our carefully formulated plans and intentions. Time management has become a major preoccupation as we struggle to cope. These days, many people seem to be motivated by a desperate, but perhaps forlorn, belief that a quieter golden age will eventually arrive, when things will calm down and when there will be time to consolidate and reclaim deeply held beliefs. The indications are, however, that the pace of change will quicken rather than slow down.

Alvin Toffler (1971) warned us a quarter of a century ago that the world was changing faster than ever before, and that the rapid acceleration of changes in all aspects of human activity would create a disorienting condition which he described as 'future shock'. He warned that unless we learn to control the rate of change, in both personal living as well as in social affairs, we are doomed to a massive adaptational breakdown. Many who have been working in the education service over the past few years might claim that such a breakdown has already occurred. Tom Peters (1988), one of the foremost chroniclers of organizational change, acknowledges this desperate need for adaptive strategies in his book *Thriving on Chaos*. He suggests that we are faced with nothing less than a revolution in organizational and management practice, a revolution that necessarily needs to challenge everything we thought we knew about managing:

> Most fundamentally, the times demand that flexibility and love of change replace our long standing penchant for mass production and mass markets, based as it is upon a relatively predictable environment now vanished.
>
> (Peters 1988: xi)

Chaos, Peters claims, is the condition we have created for ourselves through our relentless pursuit of change and development. Nothing less than a love affair with chaos will enable the managers of the future to thrive: 'Today, loving change, tumult, even chaos is a prerequisite for survival, let alone success' (p. 45).

Charles Handy (1989), writing about this world of constant change, suggests that the epoch of intent, brought in with the industrial revolution, is now over and that we have entered the 'age of unreason' in which the only prediction that will hold true is that no predictions will hold true. Observing the nature of change in recent years, he notes three factors:

1 The changes we are now experiencing are discontinuous and not part of an established pattern of change. This will be disturbing and disconcerting, particularly to those in power.

2 Small changes will be particularly significant and may make the biggest differences to our lives.
3 Discontinuous change will require discontinuous, upside down thinking to deal with it.

(Handy 1989: 5)

An environment in which fast and accelerating change is one of its most significant characteristics, poses a number of major challenges to those who manage primary schools. First, there is the general challenge – learning to live and cope with a world that is changing faster than we feel comfortable with. This is not simply a matter of increasing pace or workload, but a more fundamental challenge to self-awareness, values, beliefs and vision. We have to acquire the capacity to know what it is vital to hold on to and what to let go of. To accompany this, we will need new skills, conceptual as well as practical, in order to thrive in a world of increasing complexity and confusion.

Secondly, we face a number of more specific challenges:

• to create school cultures that are optimistic, confident and future-focused;
• to develop a curriculum appropriate to a world of constant and accelerating change;
• to prepare pupils for a world that will be significantly different from the one at present;
• to design management processes for schools that are more flexible, creative and open to continuous improvement.

In preparing for this future, four points in particular need emphasizing:

1 The pace of change will continue to accelerate.
2 Managing ambiguity, complexity and paradox will be significant challenges facing organizations.
3 Insight, awareness and understanding of human activity will be more necessary than ever.
4 The ability to thrive and survive will depend upon an increased capacity to adapt quickly to new conditions and situations.

The effective management of primary schools – indeed, of all organizations – will demand a new sense of future consciousness, a capacity to focus on the complexities of change. It will be vital to spot significant trends and tendencies and to respond to them skilfully, developing an ability to adapt and modify systems, processes and structures as changed circumstances require.

These novel conditions create a range of confusions and dilemmas for those called upon to manage the education service. The government, anxious to maintain a competitive edge in world markets, seems to be experiencing a deep confusion about how best to manage the education of the young in an increasingly fast changing and turbulent world. Its response has been to set up a series of reforms to alter the structure and content of schooling. Sadly, it has not resisted the temptation to look backwards for inspiration, to an age perceived as more certain, gentle, reassuring and successful. Nostrums from the golden age of governmental boyhoods are offered as an alternative to ideas that confront the increasingly confusing and uncertain future of which we are all part.

Most of us are all too conscious of the tangible and visible changes around us, both in our own direct experience and across the world. What we are perhaps less aware of are the internal struggles and difficulties they create for us. Seven phenomena are especially significant: pressure, complexity, ambiguity, uncertainty, confusion, turbulence and stress.

Pressure

In recent years, schools have been subjected to a range of unprecedented pressures. These can be categorized as macro pressures and micro pressures.

Macro pressures

These are the pressures that affect the whole planetary system and which are experienced across the globe. They include the rapid advances in science and technology and the enormous impact they have made on working practices and personal lifestyles: ecological changes such as global warming, atmospheric pollution and depletion of natural resources; social changes in patterns of human relationships, family life, drug cultures, unemployment and crime; political changes such as the breakdown of communist bureaucracies, the emancipation of South Africa, ethnic conflict, the movement towards a global economy and federal institutions; and the huge developments in information technology. These global pressures impact on schools in two main ways. First, they demand a curriculum which reflects these enormous trends and changes and which has the capacity to adapt quickly and flexibly to continuously changing situations. Secondly, they require schools to be a creative part of the change process itself, leading with new ideas and approaches finely tuned to emerging trends and developments. Our primary schools need to redeem the pioneering spirit that so characterized developments in primary education in the two decades after the Second World War.

Micro pressures

These are closer to home and are specific to the educational community. They are created through the steady stream of educational reforms passed into legislation over the past decade. They include structural changes such as the devolvement of school budgets through the Local Management of Schools procedure and the creation of new types of school, including grant-maintained schools and city technology colleges. The National Curriculum has created feverish waves of change to what has traditionally been taught in classrooms, significant alterations being required even before previous requirements have been fully implemented. New and tightly focused systems of evaluation and accountability have been introduced through teacher appraisal, assessment and testing and the creation of the Office for Standards in Education (Ofsted). Not only have these pressures imposed enormous extra demands on an already under-resourced service, they have diminished professional authority and created a culture of suspicion and mistrust.

These two types of pressure, in their powerful and different ways, have created a range of significant effects on the schools of the country, creating an altogether changed and changing context for the work of teachers and pupils.

Complexity

Work and organizational life is now far more complex than it ever was. The huge growth in information and data – the rules, regulations, requirements, procedures, guidelines, policies and plans that affect our lives – have vastly extended the amount of detail that is required to operate the education service. Since the regulations themselves are complicated, they need circulars, explanations and guidance documents to support them. This creates a painful dilemma – whether to try and absorb, understand and assimilate them, or to rely on efficient systems of storage and retrieval. Whichever option is adopted, more time and energy than ever before have to be allocated to the management of information and data.

Complexity has two forms. First, there is the information itself, increasing all the time and demanding an ever extending filing system to accommodate it. Computer systems are now marketed on the size of their storage capacity and their ability to process enormous quantities of data. Secondly, there are the dynamics of complexity – the human activity, both internal and external, now required to manage it and make sense of it. No sooner, it seems, than we have accommodated the most recent update, than a new one arrives to replace it. In its short life, the National

Curriculum has already been through many changes, modifications, radical revisions and updates. It is easy to blame lack of foresight. In a fast changing world, we must learn not to be surprised that further changes are already being planned before existing programmes are fully implemented. We need to adjust to shorter shelf-lives for projects and decisions, and perhaps not try to make things so perfect that they will last for ever.

Few of us were socialized or educated for complexity. The strictures in our childhoods were for simplicity and straightforwardness, always to seek the single correct solution to a problem. We were led to believe that if we think hard enough, we will be able to keep things tidy and properly accounted for. We were encouraged to seek out the main points and not worry too much about the subsidiary ones. It is frustrating not to have simple solutions, and it is only slowly dawning on us that most complex problems have complex causes, and that the search for the single most important one will probably leave the problem unsolved. Arguments about causes of crime, class size in schools and the problems of drugs become polarized by the debate between the espousers of alternative simple solutions to complexity.

We need to recognize that most issues are far more complex than we have assumed. There seems to be an assumption that all the truths about the universe and the conduct of human affairs have already been discovered. If anything, the explanations that have been created seem increasingly inadequate and incomplete to deal with the ever changing configurations of phenomena. One of the great challenges for primary school educators is how to help the children now in our schools to grow up with a capacity to manage complexity more successfully than older generations seem able to do. We must stop giving pupils simple explanations, and lead them to the acceptance of complexity and the need to see things from multiple perspectives. Those researching into complexity theory are suggesting that we need to pay far more attention to the many small variables in situations if we are to come near to a full enough understanding of the phenomena affecting our lives.

Ambiguity

During the last two decades, we have moved into an information world where meanings are often ambiguous. Language strains to sustain a capacity for clarity, as detail becomes ever more complicated and intricate. Technical language and jargon is becoming increasingly necessary to provide specificity of definition, and words in common parlance are taken to embrace particular and technical meanings. Global communication requires a common language, but until that is achieved translation will be problematical, as many of us who have struggled with translated instructions to self-assembly furniture will testify.

As the world becomes more tightly regulated and more precisely defined, more and more people will be engaged in the business of spelling things out. Regulations themselves can often be quite brief, but the guidance and interpretation that needs to accompany them can stretch to many volumes. The corrections to a recent railway timetable were longer than the original timetable itself. This means that most of us are having to allocate time from our prime responsibilities to the process of seeking clarification and understanding. And herein lies a real human predicament. Many of us have come to believe that our seeming incapacity to keep abreast of data is an indication of a significant decline in our intellectual capacities, so we tend to blame ourselves and feel ashamed of our increasingly limited abilities.

A few years ago, as this ambiguity phenomenon began to create a growing sense of discomfort, the following epithet was doing the rounds on posters and cards: 'I know you believe you understand what you think I said, but I am not sure you realize that what you heard is not what I meant'. Since a lot of documentary data are generated by people with sectional concerns and specific interests, much is detailed and technical. For those working in schools, much of the information is ambiguous, relying on previous knowledge or other documentation. This creates more work, because readers have to check out with others whether their understanding is the correct one, requiring more telephone calls, personal interruptions and time-consuming deliberation.

That we need to learn to adjust to the increasingly paradoxical and contradictory nature of life is clear. We must not blame ourselves, for if anything our powers to understand complexity and retain information in memory have improved. We are faced with nothing less than a revolution in the metabolism of meaning. It is neither possible nor desirable to try and cope with it all. We have to learn the art of skilful selectivity, and when the time comes we must learn to erase from our memories that data which is no longer useful. This will be painful and difficult learning, for most of us have experienced an education in which we were led to believe that remembering was the greatest achievement of the human species, and our successful demonstration of it in public examinations our passport to a successful future. Few, if any, of us received instructions in forgetting, of erasing items from memory.

We must learn not to be surprised by the inconsistencies we encounter in our daily lives. Complexity breeds ambiguity and creates perplexity. Perhaps it is bewilderment which is now the sign of a really first-rate intelligence. As educators, we find ourselves simultaneously struggling with the presence of ambiguity in our own lives as we try to help pupils to cope with it more imaginatively and effectively in theirs.

Uncertainty

As Charles Handy (1989) has observed, the only safe prediction is that any prediction is unsafe. Teachers were led to believe that the National Curriculum was here to stay, and so set about implementing it with energy and determination, only to discover that it was to undergo almost perpetual alteration and modification. Uncertainty about which version to use, and whether to wait until the next one arrives, has pervaded the lives of teachers. Sir Ron Dearing was called in to resolve this dilemma, but in such a rapidly changing world the whole idea of a rigidly prescriptive curriculum is questionable anyway. Constant change and adaptation will continue to be necessary, and these dilemmas will continue until the schools themselves are left to manage modification and development for themselves.

One of the characteristics of the modern world is that the predictions we were once urged to place reliance on, no longer work. It is increasingly difficult to tell our children what they can expect in their lifetimes. Life spans of over a hundred years are becoming more common and there may be children now in our schools whose lives will last from the end of the twentieth century to the beginning of the twenty-second century. What stories can we tell them about what their lives will be like in 2006 let alone 2106?

Being sure of things is another feature of our upbringing. We were educated for a world of continuity, of sequential change and a logical unfolding of events. It is no longer safe or sensible to rely on rational prediction and linear theory. It is the unexpected and the surprising which now unfold in front of us, and we feel the deep insecurity of uncertainty in our incapacity to see ahead with the confidence that we once felt.

Post-modern perspectives try to explain this 'end-of-an-era' phenomenon. They note that the characteristics of the world are now the disintegration of traditional structures and the breakdown of the big ideas that have sustained our evolution – the truth of scientific discovery, continuous economic growth, the capacity of technology to rescue us from our misguided excesses. What we are witnessing in the world of state-funded education is the fragmentation of traditional monolithic structures. The system is becoming more diverse and less subject to consistency and similarity of pattern. The difference now is that we know these changes will not last as long as the structure created by the 1944 Education Act. In the past decade, we have seen more educational legislation than in the whole previous history of state-managed schooling. The recent changes we are involved in implementing, will themselves be subject to continuous waves of alteration and modification. New ideas will need to be put in place quicker, and last shorter than before. Continuous development and improvement is the process replacing occasional change events.

In the future, we will need to place less reliance on detailed long-term plans, perhaps holding on to our value-based dreams and visions of how we want things to be while we create the plans and programmes that will get us through the next few weeks and months. This will place a new emphasis on a rather loosely defined aspect of human capability, 'living on your wits'. This will need to be introduced into the formal curriculum for schools if the adults of the future are to succeed in avoiding the debilitating effects of complexity, uncertainty and confusion. Those individuals with a capacity to work imaginatively and creatively in the moment will be the key assets of any organization. This does not imply that reckless management will replace planned development, but that we will need to attach a greater importance to the skills of managing in the heat of the moment, dealing with whole varieties of issues that no amount of planning can predict.

Fortunately, such skills have always been the stock in trade of good primary school teachers. Their work has always had a significant element of spontaneity and unpredictability about it and at their best they use their wits in a way which belies the complexity of the context in which they are managing. As yet, this cluster of abilities has defied easy description or simple analysis. We need to learn that within the elusive complexity of the primary school teacher's pedagogy lie truths about management and leadership that we need to understand and bring into the wider organizational community.

Confusion

Confusion is perhaps the single most prevalent phenomenon in most schools, and one of the greatest challenges to those in senior management positions. Few people enjoy being confused, striving to overcome their feelings of panic, disorientation, uncertainty and despair. We will need to learn to be more comfortable with the inevitable confusions that the modern world and its accelerating pace of change imposes. Although we do not like to feel confused, we are even more reluctant to confess that we are, so we wander round our schools feeling dazed while pretending to be clear.

An organization staffed with people who are pretending to know is a nightmare that can only be overcome by learning to live with confusion, and to accept its inevitable presence in our lives. Indeed, the most dangerous person in the organization of the future will be the person who claims not to be confused. In the future, it may be certainty that we need to be wary of.

The problem with confusion is partly to do with our upbringing. We learn to regard the presence of confusion in our lives as a deficiency of intellect, a weakness in our minds. People who demonstrate confusion are often referred to as 'not very bright'. Clarity and single-mindedness are regarded as the mark of a superior intelligence. No wonder so many of us struggle to conceal our confusions. The conclusion we usually come to when we experience confusion is that we are just not clever enough, and we rue the belief that if only we had worked harder at school, and payed attention to the exhortations of our teachers, we would be freed from the paralysing ineptness we so often experience. This is a most dangerous perception and one that can hold us back from a proper sense of achievement and well-being, so vital to the effective discharge of our roles and responsibilities.

If we do experience life as difficult it is because *it is*, not that we are deficient. M. Scott Peck (1985), addressing the pathologies of the modern world, begins his book *The Road Less Travelled* with an almost heretical assertion: 'Life is difficult'. He goes on to explain his thinking:

> This is a great truth, one of the greatest truths. It is a great truth because once we really see this truth, we transcend it. Once we truly know that life is difficult – once we truly understand and accept it – then life is no longer difficult. Because once it is accepted, the fact that life is difficult no longer matters.
>
> Most do not fully see this truth that life is difficult. Instead they moan more or less incessantly, noisily or subtly, about the enormity of their problems, their burdens, and their difficulties as if life were generally easy, as if life *should* be easy. They voice their belief noisily or subtly, that their difficulties represent a unique kind of affliction that should not be and that has somehow been visited especially upon them. I know about this moaning because I have done my share [original emphasis].
>
> (Peck 1985: 15)

Shifting our thinking to this more radical but reassuring viewpoint will not be comfortable. For many of us, the self-perception of inadequacy is deeply ingrained and it will not be easily relinquished.

One of the most important focuses for staff development and appraisal in the future will be to share and disclose with our colleagues the nature of our own professional dilemmas and difficulties. As the pace of change intensifies, so we will need to allocate even more specific periods of time to the vital process of deliberate reflection on our professional experience.

To accompany this we will need to accept the presence of confusion in our lives as an indication of the complexity that we are required to deal with. Confessing to confusion will come to be seen as a sign of strength rather than weakness. Perhaps only those genuinely in touch with their own confusion can claim to be living in the so-called 'real world'.

Turbulence

Some indication of the real experience of people at work can be gleaned from the metaphors they use to explain the essence of their job. Frequently employed is the notion of 'moving goalposts' – the loss of clear targets, the relentless changing of direction and priority. When a sense of purpose is absent, then inevitably purposelessness ensues. Some speak about keeping the 'plates spinning', a hard enough task when there are only a very few, a nightmare when new ones are added by the hour. Others refer to the 'increasing speed of the treadmill' and note how difficult it is to step off when the pace is fast. Most of us have found our personal lives invaded by work – tasks that cannot be undertaken in the relentless turbulence of school life, being taken home to be done when we would be better relaxing.

It is an increasingly common experience at the end of a working day to be totally exhausted but confused about what it is we have achieved. We arrive at work in the mornings with our lists of important things to do and find that by the end of the day, despite our frantic busyness, few of the items have been attended to.

Henry Mintzberg (1973), in his study of the work patterns of organizational managers, noted the turbulent complexity of their work, observing that most managers spend their time in an endless sequence of short interactions – rarely longer than eight or nine minutes – few of which they had any prior knowledge of. Most teachers, too, in the managing of pupil learning, experience this pattern with its haphazardness and unpredictability. The trouble is that we have been led to believe that good managers are proactive, successfully steering themselves elegantly through a sequence of predetermined tasks. But busy organizations, especially complex ones like schools, create a plethora of human needs which require to be satisfied if the work of the organization is to succeed. The real work of managers is to expect these wants and needs, and to respond to them vigorously and sensitively. For too long we have worked on the assumption that admitting to a need is a sign of incompetence, and so we have conspired to limit and inhabit the true potential of the organization and the creative people within it. School life is turbulent, conducted at a furious pace. Given the dynamics created by complexity, uncertainty and confusion, we have to learn that the documentary and strategic aspects of management have to be conducted when there is less turbulence and when there are more opportunities for quality time. Not an easy option for managers in the modern educational system.

Most of us are aware of this turbulence and its effects on our lives. It can be described as change that accelerates faster than our capacity to keep pace with it comfortably. It feels as if we run a constant risk of

being left behind and our inadequacies exposed to ridicule and con-
demnation because we have not tried hard enough. We are faced with
agonizing choices – work harder, faster and longer, or, as they say, 'go
to the wall'. Few deliberately choose this latter option, since they have
no investment in failure, until it is too late, and the costs of being in
overdrive for too long take their toll on our health and sanity. Sadly, it
is often the most committed and effective in our profession who end
their careers feeling exhausted and disillusioned.

It is here that the evolutionary crisis is most painfully felt. We may
know we have to adapt to survive, but few of us know what precise form
such adaptation needs to take. There is no shortage of advice – 'Work
smarter, not harder', the management gurus tell us, but they give us no
practical indication of what we should do, nor do they tell us about the
worries, anxieties and guilt that are often created when we try and give
up the habits of a lifetime. It is very hard to adopt new approaches when
those with power and influence over us are determined to judge us by
the old ones. It will take great courage to embark on this necessary process of transformation and adaptation. It is unlikely to be achieved unless
those at the top of organizational hierarchies lead by example and let go
of the assumptions, attitudes and practices that we have sustained for
too long in a changed and changing world. They will need to give the
highest priority to their own adaptation, and also provide support and
encouragement of the highest quality to their over-demanded colleagues.
The journey through the evolutionary crisis has to be led by senior staff
who recognize that it is their own working practices that may need
changing the most.

Stress

The combined effect of these features is another more insidious outcome, increased stress and psychological discomfort. Studies of occupational stress have shown teachers to be a high-risk group, and each year
an increasing number of working days are lost through stress-related
illnesses.

While some stress is a necessary prerequisite for effective human activity, it can become dangerous when individual staff members experience
a growing gap between the work they are required to do and the time
and energy required to do it in. More personal time has to be spent on
job-related activity, placing in jeopardy social well-being, family cohesion
and personal health.

For too long, occupational stress has been regarded as a matter for the
individual who experiences it, and often as an indicator of incompetence
or lack of commitment. Senior staff in schools need to recognize that
stress is a management issue and something which management processes

have the capacity to increase or reduce. The key resource for any organization is the arrival at work each day of staff who are physically fit and
healthy, energetic and optimistic and with a sense of psychological well-
being. At present, this is not true of the majority of teachers.

The combined effect of these seven phenomena is to fuel frustration,
guilt and self-doubt, dangerously sapping professional optimism, competence and ambition. Being a senior manager in this sort of social and
psychological context, when you too are experiencing similar pressures
and stresses, is not a job for the faint-hearted. Management work is becoming more and more difficult and demanding and there are no easy
fixes or quick solutions to the succession of challenges and dilemmas
that present themselves daily in the primary schools of the country. Part
of the challenge lies in the fact that, despite Toffler's warnings and the
exhortations of Peters and Handy, we have not yet adapted our cultural
and interpersonal ideas sufficiently well to cope with a world characterized by conflicts, imperatives, exhortations and a sense of unworthiness.
All our preparation and training for the management work we are now
required to do was for a different world, one with more certainties and
less confusions. Our childhood upbringing, education and training has left
us unprepared and insufficiently equipped for the world we have inherited. The only answer is to become learners again, tuned into the ambiguities and paradoxes that now so characterize the world of work and
organizations. As Peters (1992) has said in his most recent study of organizational life, 'People who are uncomfortable in an unstructured world,
won't make it'. We need to recognize that our successes and achievements as managers and leaders will depend more on what we learn
while doing the job, than what we have brought with us from the past.
The inherited beliefs, assumptions and principles which have formed the
basis for management activity since the beginning of the century have
to be challenged and confronted. Nothing short of a major shift in our
management thinking, and a fundamental change in the relationships
between senior and junior staff, is likely to produce organizational effectiveness in the increasingly complex times to come.

PANIC AND NOSTALGIA

It is unfortunate that so much of what happens in education is affected
by the competitive ethic: being brighter than someone else, getting higher
marks, achieving a landmark first. It applies in the rivalry between the
state and private sectors, and now within the state sector itself as Local
Management of Schools links school survival with pupil recruitment.
One of the common polarized arguments hinges on the belief by one

side that competition is the essence of progress, and the belief by the other that competition merely sustains inequality of opportunity and inhibits successful learning. A concern with rivalry – of winning, or at least not losing – can cloud attention to the more fundamental purposes of education.

Not succeeding in your learning has become a cause for blame. It is not so long ago, and certainly in the memory of some readers of this book, that getting things wrong resulted in some form of physical punishment. Apart from learning by fear to avoid punishment, a sense of inadequacy is instilled and low confidence in learning abilities created when we don't always get things right first time. An obsession with deficits has long been a preoccupation in the educational system and moulding us from our natural selves into 'correct' beings has been a priority for many schools.

Much change in education has had a reform element about it. The assumption that changing the structure of schooling is the way to ensure improved learning is still the belief of many politicians. While improvement is constantly required, it is sad that many of the reasons for wishing to improve are connected with tangential issues – to be better than other countries, to prove experts wrong, to increase the competitiveness of British industry, or because standards are different than they were fifty years ago. In all this there seems a reluctance to grasp the essential fact, that the world is different than it was and it is changing fast. For an educational system to be in tune with change it needs to be flexible, adaptable and responsive to constantly changing circumstances and needs.

The obsession with current deficits and difficulties does nothing to advance the idea of an educational system for a changing world. It merely deepens prejudices, further polarizes positions and keeps the debate focused on what exists now, rather than on the visions of what it will need to be like in ten or twenty years.

The solutions currently being introduced assume that the only issues that need to be taken account of are the ones that have always been taken account of; that is, those that seemed to be appropriate to a world that has passed. Imagination about change only stretches to considerations about more or less of what we have already. The rush to discover panaceas creates a tendency to retrieve discarded orthodoxies from the past, such as streaming, exclusively didactic instruction and single-technique approaches to reading.

Nowhere in the current round of reform is the notion present that the most appropriate change is continuous and systematic improvement, in which change is seen as a constant process of building and developing, rather than an event to be engaged in with great energy when things have got really bad. If schools cannot be trusted to change for themselves, then intermittent flurries of activity will be necessary. As the pace of change in the world accelerates, these flurries will become more urgent, more insistent and, sadly, increasingly dysfunctional.

One of the difficulties facing those charged with the management of schools is the rigid context for education envisaged by the reformers. Educational change is approached in strictly rational terms as a choice between opposing alternatives, only one of which is right. This manifestly fails to realize that education and learning are characterized by complexity and an infinite range of variables. Simple solutions must be at worst wrong and at best partial.

The rancorous debate about educational policy is not a fundamental exploration of ideas and possibilities about issues of learning and teaching, but a bitter and protracted argument about who is right and who is wrong. Proposals for a Royal Commission are turned down, probably because the learning that might accrue from such an exploration might be embarrassing to entrenched positions and ideologies. Once polarized on party political lines, a non-judgemental and truly independent search for ideas and possibilities becomes impossible. In addition, such explorations take time, which reforming governments do not have. Changes have to be instant, enforced and backed by centralized power.

This perpetuates the pendulum process in education, with swings one way and then the other. Either the pendulum is pushed by the political weight of legislation and regulation, or eased in the other direction as proponents begin to feel their job is done and opponents seize the day. This binary structure inhibits creative exploration and becomes an issue of winning or losing the argument. The learning process becomes the victim of politics. We are so fixed into the pattern of binary thinking that change outside this polarized dynamic becomes incomprehensible and ridiculous.

Those responsible for the direction of educational policy need to realize what an increasing number of commercial organizations have come to realize: that survival and development in a fast changing world depends upon simultaneity rather than exclusion. Polarized patterns of thinking automatically exclude certain variables and include others – the 'either/or' approach to change. Creative solutions will undoubtedly include some elements of both positions; divergence and variation will demand it. There needs to be sufficient variety of policy and practice to make development possible. Ashby's Law of Requisite Variety (Garratt 1987) suggests that for an organization to survive and develop, there must be sufficient difference within it to allow it to cope with change. The pursuit of monolithic structures will produce too much similarity, thus reducing the ability of the system to learn and adapt to a rapidly changing environment.

As the centralized and increasingly bureaucratized system becomes more rigid, it will be necessary for individual schools to have the courage of their convictions to plan for what they believe to be the best interests of pupils, parents and the community. The grant maintained option may not be pursued in order to support a political principle, but to avoid it.

One of the most dispiriting features for those involved in the running of schools is that the debate about education is conducted in a climate of dispute and discord. This sets up stresses and tensions which themselves have a debilitating effect on the process of change itself. Because issues are polarized and arguments rehearsed, there is no need to ask fundamental questions about what the basic purposes of schooling in a fast changing world are, nor to involve participants in discovering the answers and solutions.

A worrying characteristic of the debate has been the increasing tendency to denigrate educational specialists or 'experts'; that is, those who dare to offer an opinion based on first-hand experience and systematic study. It is easy to scoff at those whose influence you fear, and convenient to marginalize ideas and interpretations that jeopardize your own position. This sometimes forces the specialists to increase the vehemence of their arguments, to claim more for their research than is reasonable and to extend their generalizations into territories for which they were not destined. This further fuels the polarization within the educational community itself, creating a warfare of ideologies and entrenched positions. Just as in real warfare, it is the innocent and uninvolved who become the victims.

On the other hand, there is no escaping the fact that education is a legitimate political issue. It is naive to hope for a day when education will be freed of political intervention. Those charged with the management of educational institutions need be clear about this political reality and develop a capacity to work within its sometimes painful clutches. One way to do this is to listen to the quieter voices, particularly those of the learners themselves. It is significant that in all the documentation of the National Curriculum, not one page of it has been written and offered to the pupils. If anyone needs to know the targets for learning, it is those faced with achieving them.

Education is a synthesis, a bringing together of knowledge, ideas, possibilities and practicalities. Its very essence is experience and the meaning that is construed through reflection on it. There is very little reflection in the current debate among the protagonists. Successful change requires reflection as well as reaction, thinking as well as doing, and vision and imagination as much as intellect and belief.

ESSENCE AND APPEARANCE

Recent developments in education have emphasized performance above all things. What seems to count for most in the political debate about schooling is that pupils at each stage of their education can demonstrate formal competence on a rather narrow range of skills and abilities. It is sad that almost no attention is paid to the importance of education as an unfolding of potential, a striving for identity and understanding, and a search for happiness and fulfilment. What really seems to count most is how children behave when they are tested, not how they think or feel, or what their ambitions in life are.

This struggle between appearance and essence endangers the very process of education. At their best, primary schools have held both as self-evident, recognizing that the true education of the human being has full regard for all its potentialities. It is deeply depressing that the polarity of the traditional/progressive schism also reflects this distinction. What effective educators have always recognized is that in the process of learning, you cannot have one without the other. It is not a matter of 'either/or', but a case of elegant and appropriate synthesis.

The protracted and disputatious debate about the detail of the National Curriculum has revealed the tendency to see success as making the right choices – whether knowledge is more important than skill, design of the curriculum more important than its delivery, or structure more relevant than process. The problem lies in the creating of false dichotomies and the posing of dilemmas. These vital issues affecting the management and development of formal learning in schools cannot be reduced to questions of 'either/or'. What is needed is an acceptance that all are important and that each has an appropriate and significant contribution to make to the whole. What is equally vital is that we learn to appreciate that it is the relationships between these necessary contributory parts that holds the key to change and improvement. Until we realize that the key to understanding human affairs and activities lies more in making connections between the various factors, than in struggling to define a pecking order of relative importance, we are unlikely to satisfy our desperate need to raise the quality of learning in schools.

◆ 2 ◆ THE PARADIGM SHIFT

If, as Tom Peters (1988) suggests, we are faced with nothing less than a fundamental change in organizational and management practice, then we need to challenge everything we think we know about leadership and management. Perhaps the only way through the evolutionary crisis in the management of human affairs, is to face the possibility that we may have to give up the habits and practices of a lifetime if we are to survive. Fortunately, the seeds of this survival have already been sown, and the concept of a paradigm shift has been preoccupying researchers in a range of disciplines for over twenty-five years (Whitaker 1993).

In his book *The Structure of Scientific Revolutions*, Thomas Kuhn (1970) introduces the notion of a paradigm shift – a profound change in the thoughts, perceptions and values that form a particular view of reality. He illustrates the paradigm shift within the scientific community by describing what happens when a particular scientist deserts the rules of the paradigm and makes a discovery that does not fit within it. Since it does not fit, it has to be proved wrong. But other scientists also discover puzzling anomalies which further strain the orthodoxy. The only way out of the crisis is the creation of a new paradigm. This involves the incorporation of a principle which was present all along but has remained either undiscovered or ignored. The new paradigm is received with scepticism and some hostility and its ideas are attacked. Some established scientists remain unconverted even when confronted with overwhelming evidence. When the number of new adherents reaches a critical mass, a collective paradigm shift can be said to have occurred.

Kuhn's conceptual breakthrough in our understanding of the process of change is important, because it challenges the view that all change is a smooth and natural process. It highlights the difficulties faced by those confronting the resistance of vested interest. Since the whole notion of the paradigm is a rigid tightening around specific beliefs and ideas, change must be seen as the painful and protracted process of reinventing, reordering and redefining. This is the hallmark of a world determined to develop itself on certainty. Every time the paradigm is redefined, a belief develops that here at last is the final correct solution.

What we are now witnessing in the world of change is the struggle to devise a paradigm which is characterized by the acceptance of temporariness rather than certainty, by possibility rather than unlikeliness, and integration rather than exclusion. Such a paradigm is a departure from the pursuit of single, simple solutions to problems, to a recognition that most difficult human problems are pervaded with infinitely complex variables.

In our practice of management and leadership, we are in a state of transition between paradigms. The inheritance referred to above can be described as the mechanistic paradigm. What we are moving gradually towards is what might be called the humanistic paradigm. Essentially, this new paradigm starts with the assumption that people bring with them to school and work each day, enormous resources for the benefit and well-being of the organization, but that they need to find in the workplace a climate conducive to the willing and energetic release of these skills and abilities. One of the key challenges for educational leaders and managers is how to release the often hidden and inhibited potentialities of both staff and pupils more effectively. This will require leadership in three distinct but related areas: organizational dynamics, management structures and work culture.

SHIFTING THE ORGANIZATIONAL PARADIGM

Organizational dynamics

These are the powerful forces and ideas which determine the ways in which the organization operates. Discernible shifts in such dynamics are set out in Table 2.1.

Table 2.1 Dynamic shift factors

Mechanistic paradigm	Humanistic paradigm
Steady change	Fast change
Stability	Turbulence
Certainty	Uncertainty
Simplicity	Complexity
Rational world	Non-rational world
Rigidity	Flexibility
Autocracy	Autonomy
Separation	Integration
Delivery	Development

We are engaged in a significant shift in the forces and ideas that determine the different ways in which organizations operate. Among specific shifts is that from steady change and conscious development to constant and accelerating change. The desire for stability and the steady state will need to be replaced by an acceptance of turbulence, where simple concepts give way to unpredictability, uncertainties and ambiguities of complexity. We have to learn to let go of our conditioned reliance that the world operates according to rational and logical principles, and begin to accept and adapt to the haphazardness and confusion of a non-rational world.

These shifting forces will demand a greater capacity for flexibility as we learn to break free from the fixed and rigid patterns of the past. The autocracy of the few will make way for the autonomy of the many, if human skills and capabilities are to be optimized. Each one of us will need to rely less on our separation from one another, and more on the sharing and integration of our knowledge, skill and ingenuity. Above all, this will require organizations to change their obsession with delivery, to a commitment to curiosity and continuous professional learning and development.

The dynamic shifts outlined above will have profound implications for the ways institutions are organized and managed, and nowhere is change deemed to be more necessary than to patterns of leadership and management. These are vital if we are to create appropriate physical, social and psychological cultures for our work.

Management structures

One of the most significant factors in the paradigm shift is the appreciation that our concepts about the practice of management will have to change. Table 2.2 indicates some of the important developments already taking place in approaches to management and leadership.

Over the past decade, we have seen a gradual restructuring of management hierarchies. Flatter, more network-based structures have developed which are less status-conscious, more integrated, and capable of responding to fast changes quickly and creatively. The top-down mentality is giving way to three-dimensional, centre-out organizing. Instead of rigid and role-conscious line management, there is a developing awareness of multi-level leadership, where all members in the organizational structure have the right and duty to envision goals and lead activity towards them. Inhibiting assumptions that workers have to be commanded and controlled are making way for new beliefs and strategies which empower and enable and which build trust within the organizational culture.

Those in senior positions are having to learn that sharing power is more likely to bring organizational success than keeping it for themselves,

Table 2.2 Structural shift factors

Mechanistic paradigm	Humanistic paradigm
Hierarchy	Networks
Top-down	Centre-out
Line management	Multi-level leadership
Command/control	Enabling/trust
Exercising power	Sharing power
Dependence	Interdependence
Fixed roles	Adaptable roles
Unitary functions	Multi-functions
Task focus	Process focus
Mechanistic	Organic

bringing about a necessary and long-delayed shift from dependence within the hierarchy to interdependence across the whole organization. All of us will need to appreciate that integration, creativity and adaptability require flexible rather than fixed role definitions and single area responsibilities. There will need to be less individual responsibility and more shared responsibility in small teams and partnerships where a focus on the process of working effectively together is recognized to be as important as the traditional devotion to the task.

Developing very quickly within this paradigm shift is a recognition that the days of tightly controlled and mechanistic bureaucracies are limited, and that the time for more fluid, adaptable and organic structures has arrived. We are beginning to turn away from the damaging reductionist theories that have so dominated organizational development for the last hundred years, and to understand that organizations are not machines, but highly complex systems consisting of numerous volatile and largely unpredictable components. Management and leadership has never been so exciting and challenging.

People dynamics

Perhaps the most fundamental shift of all has been in the beliefs we hold about people, and the ways we need to be treated if organizations are to optimize human potential more successfully than in the past. A world driven only by economic and political imperatives tends to leave people feeling helpless, isolated, patronized, over-controlled and mistrusted. The costs of this are enormous. Organizations, like nation-states, are faced with the urgent but awesome task of changing the fundamental assumptions upon which human activity is organized.

Few of us enjoy being managed, but perhaps the majority of us yearn

Table 2.3 People factors

Mechanistic paradigm	Humanistic paradigm
People matter least	People matter most
People as costs	People as assets
Limited potential	Unlimited potential
Appearance	Essence
Compliance	Commitment
Behaviour	Experience
Error avoidance	Success seeking
Employees	Partners
Status	Stature

to be led – to be inspired to commit ourselves to challenges and enterprises which honour and acknowledge the skills, energy and effort which we are prepared to offer. For too long, we have sustained a world where success and achievement have been seen as the right and appropriate reward for the elite few. The majority, it has been assumed, are less able, less ambitious, less industrious, concerned only with their own material interests and with an inherent antipathy to work.

In the 1950s and 1960s, the work of a group of organizational researchers, including Abraham Maslow (1954/1970), Frederick Herzberg (1966) and Douglas McGregor (1960), revealed the enormous benefits of treating workers with respect, and of trusting their capacities for self-management and appropriate self-direction. While these ideas attracted a great deal of interest at the time, the world of organizational management was not ready for them, and they lay in abeyance until quite recently, when a concerted effort was made to discover the management practices that enhance human potential rather than inhibit it. The paradigm shift in relation to people contains some vital elements (see Table 2.3).

When people feel that they matter least, they tend to fulfil that damaging expectation, and often engage deliberately in counter-productive behaviour. Over many generations, we have perpetuated the arrogant belief that such people are like this anyway, that they were born this way, and that nothing we can do will change them. It is as if those who manage organizations have accepted withheld potential as one of the necessary costs to be borne. An increasing number of organizational managers and leaders, recognizing the appalling implications of sustaining styles of management that crush and inhibit the potential of staff, are attempting to build new and more life-enhancing organizational cultures in which understanding how people feel is as important as what they do. The compliance of workers can be transformed into commitment when people are encouraged to seek success, rather than merely to avoid making mistakes. Not until we feel partners in the organizational enterprise, rather than hired employees, will we begin to feel encouraged and motivated enough to desert traditional cautiousness and resentment for ambition and enterprise. In the future, it will not be status that we seek, but a sense of stature for who we are and what we bring to the organizational enterprise.

PRIMARY SCHOOLS AND THE PARADIGM SHIFT

Primary schools are a vital part of this changing pattern of ideas, forces and practices. Indeed, they have played a formative role in empowering the shift. It is in primary schools that we gain our first experiences of institutional and organizational life, and where we lay the foundations of attitudes, values and beliefs about how power, control and authority, as well as freedom and responsibility, are exercised in a collective setting. The educational service has also operated in the mechanistic paradigm, enforcing a rigid distinction between teaching and learning, building the underlying assumption that children do not like learning, do not want to learn and will only do so if forced, cajoled and threatened. At its worst, this paradigm has created tyrannies of oppression and inhibition.

For those currently engaged in educational leadership, the challenges are compounded. Not only do we have to transform the organizational culture in which teachers and other staff work, we also have to do it for the pupils. In many ways, recent educational reforms, particularly the Ofsted initiative, seem to be last-ditch attempts to halt the inexorable shifts in learning and teaching which were well under way before the advent of the National Curriculum. Wiser governments would perhaps have had the courage to recognize the inevitability of the paradigm shift already under way within the education community, and have provided the resources and encouragement to channel its essential vitality and energy.

The humanistic paradigm is not a soft option, nor a recipe for laxity and license. It is a highly rigorous and demanding process that will call for the best and most imaginative in us. For primary schools, it is perhaps more a question of redeeming the innovative tradition they had already established. This will be a major task in the years to come.

THE INHERITANCE FACTOR

Despite the pressures to change the schooling system, the strength of traditional orthodoxy is immense. As schools struggle to adapt to accelerating change, it is useful to consider the 'inheritance factor', the tendency to cling to structures from the past.

One of the most powerful tenets of schooling systems throughout the world is the notion of the single teacher in relation to multiple learners. It is implicit in the architecture, organization, staffing and funding of schools. There appears to be an unshakeable belief that not only is this the cheapest way to educate, but that it is the only way to educate. While there has been a gradual reduction in the pupil–teacher ratio, there does not seem to have been any attempt to challenge the basic concept, and recently we witnessed a bitter debate around the government's assertion that 'class size doesn't make a difference'. So we perpetuate a schooling system developed out of economic necessity, and inspired by the factory principle that humans are costs rather than resources, and as such the most expendable ingredient in the process.

A second inheritance is the predominance of factual knowledge in the learning process. While primary education has seen more change and development than other phases of schooling, even the most progressive of institutions have offered a curriculum which would compare closely with models that existed before compulsory education. Today, with the added factor of the National Curriculum, there is a chilling familiarity about the opening episode in *Hard Times*:

> Now what I want is Facts. Teach these boys and girls nothing but Facts. Facts alone are wanted in life. Plant nothing else and root out everything else. You can only form the minds of reasoning animals upon Facts: nothing else will ever be of service to them.
>
> (Charles Dickens 1961)

What, we may justifiably wonder, is so dangerous about 'everything else' anyway? Perhaps it is that ideas, questions, values and concerns are damaging to the *status quo*, that learners will gain knowledge above their station. Which is exactly what did happen. Mass literacy not only gave access to the Bible but also to *Das Kapital*, and we know the history of the twentieth century. Now the books that children should read are pre-scribed by the National Curriculum. Just as eastern Europe is releasing itself from two generations of prescription, the forces of change in this country seem determined to anchor developments in the past instead of in the future.

In terms of management and leadership practice, our role models go back thousands of years. One of the most significant elements in the management of communities, nation-states and empires has been the question of how those with power and resources manage the many who are not so fortunate, and who are held in subjection under them. This division in society between the powerful and the powerless, the wealthy and the poor, the possessors and the dispossessed, has been a constant feature of international politics as well as a dominating factor in the management of institutions and organizations. Within organizational settings, the hierarchical differentiation has developed over many generations with its assumptions of authority, expertise and superiority.

When we are faced with the need to change, we often feel impelled to cling on to what we know and what we are familiar with. We cite effective role models from our own pasts, noting that they managed and that, therefore, we should be able to also. What we forget is that in order to attract loyalty and admiration, the good role models in our professional history must have had to take their stand against the *status quo*. In their time they were the paradigm shifters, sometimes breaking with earlier traditions and breaking out beyond the boundaries of the familiar and expected.

The difference today is the sense of urgency that attends the need to learn new skills of flexibility and adaptation. We cannot take too long in our learning and development or we will not survive the evolutionary crisis. In some senses, an adaptational lag is already developing, and some are introducing changes to cope with a world that has already past. As educators, we must stop regarding schools as unique institutions, significantly discrete and different from all other organizations, requiring specific and particular treatment. We need to scan the whole range of institutions and the ways they are managed, and we need to look beyond the education community for our management and leadership role models, if we are to succeed in riding the inexorable waves of change that are now a constant feature of our professional lives. It is also vital that other organizations in the work community seek to learn from primary schools how they have successfully disengaged from a range of oppressive inheritance factors.

MANAGING THE PARADIGM SHIFT

One of the implications of an evolutionary crisis is that a 'business-as-usual' approach simply will not do. Survival depends upon recognizing the threats to well-being and effectiveness, and taking steps, sometimes quite radical and severe ones, to change the habits and patterns hardened over many generations. To survive the challenges to our well-being, four categories of adaptation and change are necessary: (1) conceptual change, (2) emotional change, (3) aspirational change and (4) practical change.

Conceptual change

There seems to be an obsession with the past as we move into these challenging times. Strategies like 'Back to Basics' strive to recapture the apparent ease and elegance of earlier times. Such management by nostalgia is bound to be thwarted, since the circumstances that we want to apply previous basics to have changed, and will continue to do so. It is time to stop seeing the future simply as a linear development of the past.

Among some of the most cherished assumptions, drummed into us from early childhood, are those to do with perfection and the need to get things right first time. The proverb 'If a job is worth doing, it is worth doing well' has been one of the conditioning factors in our approach to work. With the pace of change accelerating so quickly, we can no longer afford the luxury of a detailed, cautious and painstaking approach to many tasks. New ways of thinking need to condition our approach. Perhaps the first question to ask is, 'What will the consequences be if we do absolutely nothing about this?' It is surprising how much work that is undertaken is not necessary at all, or adds only marginally to effectiveness and quality. A great deal of energy and time is wasted in attending to things which are best left. A new proverb is needed: 'If a job is not worth doing well, it's not worth doing at all'. If under intolerable workload pressure some pieces of work eventually fall by the wayside, simply because there is neither the time nor the capacity to deal with them, then it is better that the decision to abandon is made early. Hanging on to pieces of work and feeling guilty about not attending to them is an unnecessary cause of frustration and stress.

One of the purposes of careful planning is to anticipate the potential difficulties and problems that may arise in the course of a project. We must stop believing that we can anticipate all possible problems and plan for them. We will need to turn new ideas into action quicker than ever before, for situations will emerge which will require their early modification. We cannot afford the luxury of long lead-in times. We need new concepts such as 'good enough plans' rather than perfect ones, 'fitness for purpose' rather than excellence against all standards, and 'relative to available resources' rather than reaching beyond ourselves by efforts we cannot comfortably afford.

Similarly, we need to check our attitudes to change. We must not always rush into defensive postures when it becomes necessary to move out of the temporary comfort of the familiar. We are now part of a profession whose *raison d'etre* is learning for change. We are perhaps the first generation of educators who cannot predict with any security what the circumstances of our pupils' lives are likely to be in the future. Not only is it dangerous to make forecasts about twenty years ahead, it is unwise to risk them for even a few years into the future.

It will be necessary to stop regarding change as an event that will require strenuous efforts from time to time, but change as a process of continual adaptation and modification. Development will become a process of continuously small but significant improvements, rather than occasional all-out efforts. This will require a new alertness to circumstances, and a capacity to change things as and when required. We will need greater degrees of trust between management partners and an increased capacity for what Tom Peters and Robert Waterman (1982) described as 'simultaneous loose/tight properties'. The primary schools of the future will need tight control of the values, visions and principles of their work, but individuals within the system, both pupils and teachers, will need greater authority to work with trust and integrity within their own spheres of influence. This will necessitate a reworking of traditional roles and responsibilities, spreading authority traditionally residing at the top of the organizational hierarchy throughout the school, and pupils too, will need to have a much greater part to play as co-managers of the process. The principle of subsidiarity – ensuring that decisions are taken at the lowest possible level – will form a key part of the primary school of the future.

One of the most vital conceptual adaptations needed is future-focused thinking. We must spend more time and energy looking ahead rather than behind. We need to see both where things are going and where they are coming from. Spotting tendencies and anticipating trends will become the stock in trade of the successful twenty-first century manager. Future focused thinking will need to feature in all levels of primary school leadership, including curriculum coordination, pedagogic development and school organization. It will also need to become a central feature of the learning process itself, enabling pupils to develop an early facility in change management.

Writing about the need to give pupils in schools a future focus in their learning, David Hicks and Catherine Holden (1995: 10) make a distinction between learning about the future and learning for the future:

> ... teaching *about* the future does nothing to prepare students actively for a tomorrow that will be different from today. It merely tells them what might happen. Education *for* the future, on the other hand, requires exploration of their own and others' hopes and fears for the future and the action required to create a more just and ecologically sustainable future [original emphasis].

While this has major significance for us as classroom educators, it also has implications for us as management developers. What these authors are proposing is that adaptation is not only a response to changed circumstances, but a real attempt to change those circumstances in our lives which we are not prepared to sustain. The future is not inevitable, and we do not have to be the unwilling victims of it. The future of primary school education is what we make it, and what we are prepared to do to introduce more powerful and effective ways of helping the pupils in our schools to engage effectively with an increasingly uncertain future.

Emotional change

Recently, an increasing tension between the personal and the professional dimensions of life has developed in the teaching profession. As pressure and complexity have increased, there has been a greater tendency than in the past to blur the boundaries between these two important aspects of our lives. Reports about occupational stress note the tendency for many groups of workers to undertake a significant proportion of their work at home, and many teachers find themselves working most evenings and for a significant part of their weekends. While there will need to be practical solutions to this seemingly inexorable invasion of our personal and family lives by our professional activity, it is also important to understand the psychological elements in this emerging tension.

There is an inherited assumption that as we cross the threshold from home to work we must put aside the worries and concerns of our personal lives and concentrate on the job in hand. In the past, this was not always easy, but most were able to handle it most of the time. Today, as the boundaries become more ambiguous, and the combined impact of our struggles to lead full and satisfying lives becomes more pronounced and confusing, it is necessary to build new assumptions about the relationship between home and work. It is no longer appropriate to accept that our personal experience of living in a complex, confusing and uncertain world is a matter for lonely and individual struggle. The tensions of school life and the pressures of professional responsibility and accountability need to become legitimate and necessary issues for the organization as a whole. Stress is heightened in significantly changed circumstances, and its presence in our lives is of concern to all, particularly to those with senior responsibility for the organization and management of our work.

In Chapter 1, a distinction was made between two aspects of our personal world: the outer world of appearance and performance and the inner world of essence and experience. We seem to be struggling to keep up appearances in our professional work, while at the same time concealing considerable frustration, confusion, guilt, anger and resentment within ourselves. Breakdowns occur when we can no longer sustain this deception. There is a painful tendency to blame ourselves for the seeming incapacity to keep abreast of ever increasing workloads. We do not take seriously enough the fact that we are faced with novel situations and unreasonable demands. We have to realize that if we are finding life difficult, then it is because it is.

The stress is compounded because we have no proper outlet for these inner pressures and painful emotions. We look at others and they seem to cope, but they too are keeping up appearances and struggling to sustain the approval of those whose good opinions they depend upon for professional self-esteem. A whole new approach to the management of work is required, where an emphasis on professional development is accompanied by a serious concern for personal welfare and well-being. It is in the best interest of any organization to have physically fit and emotionally healthy, as well as professionally competent, workers. We are in danger of destroying psychological health and reinforcing emotional disease. The complexities of teaching and managing require us to be at our best – physically, emotionally and intuitively. We can longer leave an appropriate sense of well-being to individuals to manage for themselves. Stress is created in and by the pressures of organizational life, and it is in organizational setting that it needs to be dealt with.

Aspirational change

Another significant shift in the management paradigm is from obedience to external control, to a proper inner-directed ambition for the school, its pupils and staff. Most teachers are motivated by dearly held beliefs and values about their work and have an enormous commitment to the present and future lives of the pupils they teach. Recent regulations have stolen the driving force of educational development from the profession and placed it in the hands of regulatory bodies whose place and experience is outside schools. If a proper balance of accountability and influence is to be achieved for the educational system, some power and authority needs to be redeemed by those working within schools.

An obsession with the school development plan has focused attention on the detail of programmes and activities. In the future, with faster change and shorter-term plans, greater emphasis will need to be placed on the loftier elements of aspiration and ambition. Underpinning any plans for development need to be dearly held values and beliefs, and clearly articulated principles and visions. These will provide the energy and motivation for a schooling process vital to the creation of optimum conditions for a future society. If we focus on the future only through prosaic and pedantic levels of attainment targets and programmes of work, then we diminish the higher talents of our educators and their pupils. We need to promote greater attention to professional dreams and visions, and engage in the sharing of educational philosophies and beliefs so that we can articulate a set of foundation principles upon which our work in primary schools can be built.

Practical change

All of these shifts will require practical adaptation. We will need to stop doing some things we have always done, and start doing other things we have never done before. And we will have to do less of some things in order to do more of others. Nothing less than a thorough overhaul of all our assumptions about teaching and learning, our beliefs about what constitutes a good school and our ideas about what characterizes effective leadership, will be enough. Tinkering around produces a repair. What we need is a significant rebuilding.

In their illuminating analysis of the current predicaments faced by staff in schools, Michael Fullan and Andy Hargreaves (1992: 51) emphasized the importance of an inner driving force: 'What is worth fighting for is not to allow our schools to become negative by default but to make them positive by design'. What this means in practice is that security and confidence about what a school does will not depend upon satisfying the somewhat rule-of-thumb criteria of an inspection system that at best expresses personal opinions about practice, but upon the capacity to build the trust, support and confidence of those who have a real stake in the school and its future. Ambitious teachers, involved pupils, supportive parents and committed governors can unite to build that solid confidence and sense of endeavour from which enterprising development can spring. External observation expressed only through such terms as 'sound' and 'satisfactory' can do little to assist the process of continuous school improvement that the government is so anxious to secure. As the exponents of total quality management proclaim, 'it is only the customers who can decide whether quality has been achieved'.

THE LEARNING ORGANIZATION

In the face of rapid and accelerating change, it is increasingly necessary to see learning in the organizational context as well as at the individual level. The phrase 'the learning organization' is a strongly emerging concept. Bob Garratt (1987: 10) argues that learning has become the key development commodity of an organization:

> Generating and selling know-how and know-why, the learning of the organization and its people, is becoming the core of any organization which has the chance of surviving in the longer term. We already know a lot about organizational learning processes. When this is added to the new ideas on the generation of vision, the refinement of thinking processes, the development of policy and strategy, the notion of managing as a 'holistic' process, and the acquisition of new managerial skills from outside the traditional boundaries, then there is a powerful mix available.

It is to such a powerful mix that Peter Senge (1990) attends in his book about the learning organization. In *The Fifth Discipline*, he suggests that learning organizations are the ones which have destroyed the illusion that the world is created of separated and unrelated forces. He proposes

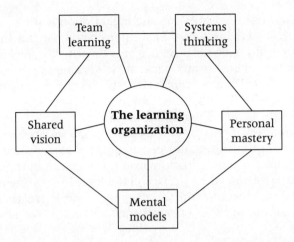

Figure 2.1 Core disciplines for developing a learning organization.

five learning disciplines which will converge to create powerful and effective organizations of change: systems thinking, personal mastery, mental models, shared vision and team learning (see Fig. 2.1).

Systems thinking

This is the overarching discipline for seeing wholes, patterns and relationships of change. It looks for the structures that underlie complex situations and involves a shift of mind and thinking (see Table 2.4). Systems thinking involves all the participants in an organization sharing responsibility for the problems generated by a system, and for developing the creative solutions to them.

Personal mastery

The learning organization will be one that transcends the traditional organizational assumptions about human potential and which recognizes that people are the active force in the pursuit of organizational aims, with a wealth of energy, skill and talent available for realizing them.

Table 2.4 Systems thinking

From	To
Seeing parts	Seeing wholes
Seeing people as helpless victims of change	Seeing people as active participants in change
Reacting to the present	Creating the future

A key characteristic of the learning organization is the recognition by leaders of the 'sacredness of their responsibility' for the lives of their people. Supporting individual participants to strive for personal mastery involves helping them to approach their working life from a creative rather than a restrictive viewpoint. It embodies the process of continual clarification of what is important, and learning how to see current reality more clearly, as an ally and not an enemy.

Personal mastery stems from a dynamic relationship between vision (a clear picture of a desired future) and purpose (a specific driving force towards it). This can create structural conflicts between the tensions drawing individuals towards their goals, and the forces anchoring them to traditional beliefs and values. The learning organization creates a relentless willingness to root out the ways in which we limit or deceive ourselves from seeing what really is.

Mental models

The future, Senge (1990) suggests, will require us to abandon our reliance on linear and vertical thinking as the chief sources of mental activity. Creativity and the greater use of imagination and intuition will need to balance our traditional obsession with rationality and logic. Increasing reliance will need to be placed on the use of reflection and enquiry skills, particularly those that enable us to challenge the assumptions that hinder and inhibit the building of creative scenarios for change. Far from being private and personal possessions, our mental models will need to be more open to enquiry and comment from our colleagues so that we can avoid what Chris Argyris (1982) calls 'skilled incompetence', that capacity to protect ourselves from the pain and threat posed by new learning situations.

Building shared vision

The learning organization is one that engages in the active process of envisioning, a collaborative activity to design and describe the future that reflects the collective aims and aspirations of those making up the organization. In this sense, vision needs to be seen as a calling rather than simply a good idea. Shared vision can uplift people's aspirations, create sparks of excitement, compel experimentation and risk-taking, and increase the courage to succeed. Shared vision can never be 'official', it needs both to bubble up the organization as well as to filter down, connecting personal visions in an elaborate tracery of ambition and purpose. Vision is not to be seen as a solution to problems, but rather a driving force for the process of co-creation. It is the central element of leadership work, relentless and never ending. It involves constant attention to three key questions:

1 What does the future we are seeking to create look like?
2 Why are we pursuing this particular vision?
3 How do we behave to be consistent with the vision we are committed to?

Team learning

Learning organizations have recognized for some time that collaboration together with a proper individualism is the key source of dynamic strength for development. An increasing tendency to tackle work through task groups and temporary teams requires attention to the processes of collaboration as well as to the work itself. This requires a focus on collective learning if the potential of participants is to be harnessed effectively. There will need to be an enhanced capacity to use conflict creatively, to use dialogue rather than discussion to root out defective thinking habits and defensive routines. The process of action learning, involving team members using the experience of the work itself as the chief source for improvement, will need to become a way of life.

These five learning disciplines, Senge (1990) argues, will converge to create powerful and effective learning organizations. While developing separately, each will prove critical to the others' success, just as in any effective ensemble. Each provides a vital dimension in building organizations that can truly learn and enhance their capacity to realize their highest aspirations. Success and achievement will depend upon certain characteristics being developed:

1 A shift from an instrumental to a sacred attitude to work.
2 A community where mutual support replaces individual exploitation.
3 A covenant between the individual and the organization as opposed to a contract.

The learning organization is one that is geared to change and determined to develop and refine its capacities to move into the future with confidence, curiosity and commitment.

The paradigm shift, and the five disciplines outlined above, are of enormous significance to the successful future of primary schools. But it is important to note that primary schools were early exponents of the paradigm shift, and many of the developments now being introduced into business organizations are at the heart of primary school life. Primary schools are well placed to lead the evolutionary journey in organizational development, using their undoubted strengths and qualities as springboards to the effective and life-enhancing organizations they have the potential to become.

◆ 3 ◆ ACHIEVEMENT AND POTENTIAL

THE ORGANIZATIONAL WORLD

Primary schools are one of our most familiar organizations. Like the local shop or parish church, there is one in most villages and neighbourhoods, and almost all of us have spent some years as a member of one. It is sad, therefore, that they have featured little in the literature on organizations. Indeed, there is a tacit view that schools lie outside the boundaries of organizational theory and do not need managing. The tendency to think of schools as separate from the general community of organizations says something about our social attitudes to learning, as well as our values about the role of children and teachers in society. It is as if their predominantly child population debars primary schools from serious attention: that anything to do with the pre-adult world is somehow frivolous, is best left to women and does not need to be taken seriously. How sad it is that perhaps most people working in the non-educational mainstream of organizations would regard as ridiculous the idea that primary schools have much to demonstrate about effective management and leadership.

This tendency to ignore, or at least to marginalize, the pre-adult world is dangerously negligent in a society which needs all the good ideas it can get. If we want to understand more about how and why people behave as they do when they are adults, it is sensible to note what happens to them when they are children. Primary schools are ideal places in which to study the concept of organization, to observe how young children react to their first experiences of institutional life, how they respond to controlling forces other than those provided by their parents, and how they make the decisions about how to manage their personal needs, their developing relationships and their educational potential.

It is not only in the primary school that children undergo their first experience of planned and organized education, but it is also the first time they encounter that most powerful of social structures – organizational life. The transition from home to school is one of the most significant rites of passage in early childhood; for four- and five-year-olds, often more significant and traumatic than later ones will be. That children manage it so well is a tribute to their frequently underestimated powers of understanding and adaptation, and their capacity for sensible self-direction. By lunchtime on their first day at school, most children have sorted out a whole of range of regulations and requirements, gained a sense of the sources of power in the organization, learnt about possible danger points to be avoided and made some new friends with whom to share all these new experiences.

The social world

Although the implementation of the National Curriculum has temporarily suspended the natural and organic development of primary schools, we continue to learn about the symbiotic relationship between the educational and social functions of the primary school. Recent government pronouncements have attempted to minimalize the vital social element of schooling, and have significantly underestimated the role that primary schools play in helping children to become sturdy, independent people and responsible citizens. One of the main propositions of this book is that unless children are helped and encouraged to fulfil themselves during the primary phase of their schooling, they are unlikely to be able to do it successfully later.

At the time of writing, the debate about the organization of pre-school education rages. Vouchers are seen as the means by which children can begin to hone their vital cognitive powers. What seems to be left out of the discussion is the vital element of social living that nursery education has always been so concerned with. It is often in the classrooms of a good nursery school that you see these two important elements – the social and the educational – optimally combined. Four-year-olds can show us, if we care to watch them and to take them seriously, what it means to be an active learner and a responsible citizen.

Leadership and management

Leadership is a concept in management theory that tends to focus on the most senior and powerful members of large corporations. What sensitive and alert observers of good primary schools will discern, are a whole range of subtle and effective forms of leadership at work, leadership that helps the children themselves to consider big ideas and relate them to their developing world view, that encourages rather than cajoles, that arouses rather than imposes, and that kindles rather than enforces. What we rarely see in these places is leadership which arbitrarily imposes its own will, that underestimates the potentialities and aspirations of its participants, and which patronizes the small size and young age of its members.

It is sad that so few teachers regard themselves as rightful members of that occupational group referred to as 'managers'. Teaching has seldom been equated with managing, and many would take the view that teaching is a more straightforward and less demanding activity than that conducted by most business managers. This is a very short-sighted view. If we see 'managing' as getting things done with and through people, then undoubtedly teachers are engaged in the process of managing. What we see in the primary school is something even more enterprising and exciting: pupils as managers, exercising levels of self-direction, responsibility and accountability that they may never experience in their later careers.

If we wish to help our schools to develop effectively in the fast changing world, then we need to realize and appreciate their significance as complex organizations, faced with the most formidable of tasks – the bringing of young people to a relevant and appropriate state of readiness to take on the awesome responsibilities of adult life. We will need to take a more lively interest in the power of primary schools to inform us about the skills of building safe and nourishing organizations, and to reveal the sorts of management and leadership expertise that many business organizations would be proud to possess.

RICHNESS AND INTENSITY

As organizations, primary schools offer their participants, both adults and children, an enormous variety of rich and intense experiences. During their primary school lives, children undergo six years of extensive self-development and change. They enter school, each the centre of an enclosed but complex social world, and leave with levels of knowledge, skill and understanding infinitely more sophisticated and advanced than their equivalents only a generation ago. During this time, they grapple with the enormous demands of the National Curriculum; they witness their parents' almost neurotic desire for them to be better than everyone else; they form, mould, discard and develop relationships and friendships; and they struggle to make sense of the inordinate contradictions present in their complex world.

For pupils, the primary school years are the ones where they begin to discover the nature of their humanity, to develop a sense of what it means to be a person and to learn what needs to be done to experience self-esteem, confidence, achievement and a sense of belonging. It is in the daily round of family life, and in the more varied and larger structures of the primary school, that they begin to experiment with behaviours, reflect on the meaning of their experiences, and place in some sort of conceptual framework the complex and often mysterious phenomena of their lives.

Spontaneity

For teachers, in addition to the formidable challenge of the National Curriculum, there is the inevitable and unrecognized commitment to the social dimensions of learning and growing. There are the surprising and frequently unpredictable responses of children to the experiences which are provided for them, as well as the awesome challenge of relating to so many children at a distinctly personal, individual and private level. Perhaps above all, there is the excitement of presiding over the process of learning and growth itself, more elusive now that classroom life has become so hidebound and constrained by an over-demanding commitment to narrow knowledge-based education. Although they may yearn for more stability and a less volatile pace of change, primary school teachers have no investment in a quiet life. They are often at their best and most effective amidst the unpredictability and demanding spontaneity of classroom life. They live constantly with potential disorder, but such are their skills that classrooms tend to be calm, purposeful and creative places.

This constant tension between order and chaos is a rich feature of primary school life. The potential for social disorder in a primary school is enormous, yet virtually all our primary schools are well managed and orderly places where children spend the majority of their time in purposeful endeavour. This has long been so, yet school development planning runs the danger of becoming something which is pursued for its own sake, rather than as the means to optimize potential. It seems that we are being forced to return to the principles of scientific management proposed by Frederick Taylor (1947) in the first half of this century – raising prediction and definition to pre-eminence in an unpredictable and ambiguous world.

Much of successful learning, and indeed effective leadership, arises out of the moment – something happens and something has to be done about it. So demanding now are the bureaucratic processes that inevitably accompany overtight planning and accountability based on mistrust, that teachers are finding themselves dreading the unexpected and serendipitous moments of classroom life that they once loved so much, and relied on to bring realism and relevance to their classroom work. The curriculum is now an ordered model of the world in which there are no rainbows, no times for sadness shared, few moments of fun and little exhileration. Today the curriculum seems to be more important than the learners for whom it was designed.

Pupils in primary schools are the raw material for the teacher's art. Few other organizations can claim such a rich resource for the practice of their professionalism. Good teachers have always demonstrated a subtle capacity to reconcile two significant elements of classroom life – the common elements which all pupils demonstrate, and the unique elements which only individuals display. If we err too far along the lines of the first, we end up with rigidity, regimentation and drill; too far along the other and we create separation, disconnection and chaos. It is unfortunate that one of the lessons society seems to have drawn from history is that people are most obedient when they are dominated, controlled and regulated. One of the finest aspects of the primary school tradition is the way in which teachers help pupils to combine a sense of togetherness as a class while sustaining a sense of individuality. Primary teachers are amazingly knowledgeable about their pupils, holding in their memories far more data about learning than any assessment procedures are likely to determine. This capacity to serve the interests of individuals simultaneously with the needs of the class as a whole is a rare skill, seldom seen with such gentle command in other sorts of organization.

Differentiation

Differentiation is recognized as one of the great challenges in a system which regards the teaching of thirty or so children in a class with a single teacher as the best way to organize state-managed education. We have come to regard the fact that children come into school as individuals different from each other as a problem to be solved, rather than as an advantage to be seized. The schooling system has gone to enormous lengths to overcome this difficulty. Age-specific learning has become one of the established nostrums of the schooling process and streaming has been tried, often at enormous costs to personal and social well-being.

We have become obsessed with the need to produce the same knowledge, the same levels of skill, the same patterns of behaviour in all children, and we stuff them into uniforms to reinforce this fear of difference and individuality, claiming that it helps children to learn more effectively. It is almost as if we fear learning, regarding it as a force to be subdued rather than as a birthright to be honoured. Yet mixed-age learning has always been a significant feature of primary education, and children from small village schools are as well represented in the high-status roles in our society as those who attended larger schools with single-age classes.

Subtlety

At their best, primary schools have understood subtlety. As a society we have tended to be far too simplistic about what is good for children. Primary educators seem to have some instinctive feel for the complex balances which need to be struck if children are to learn effectively and grow in confidence and ambition. The balance between order and disorder, trust and control, freedom and responsibility, all ideas which tax the most imaginative of governments, are often seen to be handled with light and dextrous touches in the primary school classrooms of this country. It is a matter of balance and proportion. It is in primary schools that many of us were encouraged to develop our innate capacity for self-direction and self-regulation. Good primary school classrooms produce the best features of a civilized society: a respect for self and others, a sense of wonder and curiosity, a tendency for cooperation and shared endeavour, and a commitment to high levels of aspiration and achievement. These factors seem to emerge best when the social and psychological environment is rich in sensitivity, support and understanding.

Unpredictability

Recent government-directed changes in schooling have stressed the mechanistic and rational: school development plans, attainment targets, paper-and-pencil tests and league tables. Most primary school teachers know how unsafe and unwise it is to ignore the more elusive, complex, unpredictable but enormously significant and important elements of the schooling process. They tend to resist the simplistic assumption that primary schools are microcosms of a rational world that can be ordered and contained by design. Child-centred approaches to primary education have often been accused of being sloppy and undemanding. The view that academic achievement by the young can only be sustained through rigidity, tightness, rigour and discomfort is very slow to die, despite a wealth of evidence against it.

Perhaps what we have lacked as a profession is a clear explanation of the awesome complexities of the learning process and the almost impossible demands of channelling the varied capacities of young learners in identical directions. It is time for these varied elements to be identified and more clearly articulated. Fortunately, there is a collective wisdom available for this task – the teachers in our primary schools who are a hugely underestimated resource for effective development. If, instead of blaming schools for the difficulties in society, the government had confessed its panic, anxiety and confusion about state-managed education and invited teachers to join a rigorous and well-managed development task force for the management of our schools over the next twenty-five years, what a flowering there might have been, what a richness of experience to share and develop, what possibilities might have been grasped.

DISTINCTIVE FEATURES

Diversity

While the 'one-form entry' primary school has been described as the ideal, the British system has supported enormous diversity. Indeed, there are still a significant number of very small primary schools, mostly in rural areas. In some local authorities, a significant proportion of schools have eighty pupils or less. At the other extreme, there are also some very large schools with eight hundred pupils or more.

Such diversity presents a range of challenges that professional training does not always anticipate and prepare its future teachers for. While the National Curriculum prescribes uniformity of content and intended outcome, the teachers in our primary schools are faced with a bewildering variety of contexts, situations, circumstances and environments. A single-age class in a depressed downtown location where there are a dozen or so different home languages, contrasts considerably with a mixed-age class of children who live on farms and have been born to the land. It is a tribute to the work of primary schools up and down the country that such divergence produces such consistency.

Climate and ethos

One of the very great delights of primary schools is their capacity to create a nourishing context for learning and growth. The teachers of our very youngest children have long known the supreme importance of partnership with parents, and the process of building safe bridges between the home and the school has been a significant development in primary education over the last decade or so. It is this vital sensitivity to the psychological as well as the physical needs of children that has been such a distinctive feature of British primary education. Overseas visitors to our schools are often surprised at the intimacy that is forged between primary school children and their teachers. The visionary pioneers of early childhood education in this country knew how important these relationships are, and advocated a view of education which was based on unfolding the potential for growth rather than implanting requirement and regulation. The skilful ways in which primary teachers balance the complex tensions between sensitivity to individual needs and the social imperative of inculcating values and behavioural norms is often quite staggering.

It is this child-centredness which has been at the heart of primary school development for half a century now. Yet the very phrase seems to send a shiver down the spines of reactionaries, who believe that harsh regimes, no-nonsense discipline and a good degree of emotional deprivation are the conditions under which children learn best. Having entered the blood stream of politicians, this view has enabled decades of thoughtful and careful, if sometimes over-exuberant, development to be checked. One Secretary of State went so far as to say that teachers who cared more for their children's welfare than their learning performance were guilty of the most pernicious dogma. Such over-simplifying of complex processes has certainly been responsible for a crisis of pedagogy. Yet rather than raise a debate about the intricate relationship between learning and teaching, the government bombarded the profession with the smoke screen of curriculum change, believing that if you get the content right, then the pedagogy will take care of itself.

While teachers have floundered under the weight of curriculum bureaucracy and have felt the dreadful and totally unwarranted attacks upon their integrity, they have not wavered in their belief that the successful development of young children depends upon a subtle and complex mix of variables. They know that to ignore the emotional and psychological needs of children as they engage in the process of learning is to miss the point entirely. It is this systemic complexity which is at the heart of primary school life. Because the learning process is so complex, it is difficult to articulate without appearing simplistic. Academic researchers who spend their lives observing and enquiring in primary schools have not yet succeeded in understanding and explaining fully the enormous range of variables that affect a child's capacity to learn successfully in an organizational setting.

Flexibility

Such complexity demands considerable flexibility. One of the most distinctive features of good teaching in primary schools has always been the important balance between preparedness and extemporization. In observing teachers at work in primary schools, it is fascinating to note the skilful and sensitive ways in which they switch between these two modes. It is perhaps best described as the art of skilful simultaneity – that is, holding two distinct purposes in mind (pupil welfare and curriculum progress) and being able to serve each in order to promote both. This is very much what primary school teachers are doing moment by moment as they manage classroom life, although two ideas held simultaneously is something of an underestimate. It is the essence of this process that deserves much more attention in our professional development and classroom-based research.

If attention to these processes was not enough, primary school teachers also need to demonstrate an 'all-subject capacity'. In the primary school, specialism does not only imply more extended knowledge of a subject, but also an understanding of how that subject can be managed in ways that sustain connections across the whole curriculum and do not produce dessication and fragmentation in children's minds. It is the responsibility of each teacher to devise a strategy that enables all children to learn in all curriculum areas to the optimum of their capacity. Here we are faced with another challenging balancing act – the need to keep knowledge and understanding sufficiently integrated so as to relate meaningfully to the emerging world-views of young pupils, while at the same time making progress in subject areas which over time have developed distinctive disciplines of their own. This requires yet another form of skilful simultaneity, producing the need for deliberate pedagogic precision and intuitive extemporization. It is the challenge of engaging in definition on the one hand and supporting insight and discovery on the other. At its best in the hands of good teachers, the subtelty of this balance can be both breathtaking and beautiful.

It is this demanding process of balancing that is such a distinctive feature of primary education. It is not that teaching in the later phases of schooling is easier, but rather that it is different. As children get older and gain more experience of the learning process, it is easier to engage with them in determining what works. In the primary school years, children's minds are a flurry of activity, working overtime to form themselves into serviceable and life-enabling tools. One of the key questions for primary school teachers is how the curriculum can serve to unfold the manifest mysteries of human life for children as they become more aware of its ambiguities and inconsistencies on a daily basis. What we tell them about the world is not always how they experience it. It is the role of the primary school teacher to preside over this vital and endlessly fascinating process.

ORGANIZATIONAL FORMS

In the recent debate about education, very little attention seems to have been paid to the factors that affect learning when it takes place in an organizational setting. The psychological and social dynamics of classroom life have a significant impact on the capacity of children to learn effectively, and upon the ways teachers carry out their professional roles. Success and failure in the system can be affected by the complex variables of organizational life and the extent to which these add to, or inhibit, the learning potential within each individual pupil. The government seems satisfied that the only expedients necessary to raise standards are to release schools from local authority control, prescribe a knowledge-based curriculum with mechanistic measures of performance, and devise an inspection system built on fear and retribution. When commercial businesses need to improve, it is to the organizational dynamics that they often turn first in the search for explanations of under-performance.

Traditionally, very little attention has been paid to these organizational factors, and their neglect in the overall management of the schooling system is a significant omission. Schools with their systems of rules and regulations, values, standards, expectations and patterns of belief, are the child's first experience of institutional life. To succeed in organizational life, we not only need to know and understand how these systems operate, but also how they can be used to satisfy our needs and serve appropriate self-interest. Feeling comfortable with the human culture of an organization can help to release energy, enthusiasm and enterprise. Feeling alien to organizational norms can create frustration, depression and despair. The emerging assumption within the educational world seems to be that schools are predetermined organizations, to which pupils and teachers are required to adapt. If either pupils or teachers feel uncomfortable, then it is the fault of the individual and not of the system.

Because schools are not businesses in the traditional sense, they have not featured very much in the literature on organizations. Despite this omission, primary schools have made a significant contribution both to the development of organizational forms themselves and to our understanding of them. They have resisted attempts to make them solely functional in educational terms, recognizing that to neglect human needs and to cater for the delicate and gradual unfolding of personality and potential is a responsibility which cannot be ignored. At their best, primary schools have been wonderful examples of integrated organizations serving social, emotional and psychological needs as well as purely educational ones. Perhaps we are now at a stage in our organizational history when they will be used as an important focus for research, and as models for those in the wider business community who desire to create more humanly focused organizations.

OPTIMISM AND AMBITION

The post-war history of primary education has reflected the special factors connected with the age range it serves. By the end of primary school, a child's journey to maturity and adulthood is at about the half-way stage. Primary educators have long argued that unless this particular phase is successfully negotiated, then the ultimate destinations will be difficult to reach.

What we witness in secondary schools, as children enter and engage in adolescence, is the difficult and often painful struggle for identity and meaning. If too much of their earlier agenda is left unattended to, and children enter their teens with significant unfinished business from childhood, then the growth process can be seriously hindered, causing frustration, confusion and the accompanying self-doubt.

It is in the earliest years of life that we witness the awesome potential of personhood and what it means to be human. Newly born babies demonstrate human activity at its most purposeful and intense – striving, ambition, strategy, resistance, enthusiasm, curiosity, distress, need, energy, contentment, poise, relaxation and reflection. No wonder adults love to gaze into prams. It is this integrative intelligence, as yet undifferentiated, that gives babies such life, such vibrance and such fascination. Freud summed it up well: 'What a distressing contrast there is between the radiant intelligence of the child and the feeble mentality of the average adult' (Freud, quoted in Bly 1990: 7).

In these very early years of a child's life, adults pay great attention to appearance and behaviour – walking, talking, eating and excretion. It is as if what they see and witness is the whole of our life, rather than only a part of it – the visible part. The greater part, perhaps the most important part, is within us, some of it secret and undetectable. While it is the natural tendency for us to learn to share this inner world with the adults around us, we come to understand very early that it can be dangerous to do so, and so we withhold what we perceive to be our darker secrets, our shameful thoughts, our disgusting ideas, our dreadful tendencies. And so develops a significant split in the management of our lives – the inner and the outer, what people can see and hear, and what we keep to ourselves.

The primary school years are concerned with the delicate and gradual process of unfolding potential, and channelling it productively in the child's best interests. We have perhaps taken that interest as too much of a known, claiming that we do know best what is good for a child. Perhaps we have not learnt to make the distinction between what is best and what feels best. The imposition on children of seemingly arbitrary decisions can at best be bewildering, at worst dangerous. As adults we have been trained over the generations to put appearances above experience, to have no truck with wilfulness in children. We rarely stop to ask that most vital of questions: What is happening inside the child for it to behave in this way?

Most of us survive the scars and traumas of the undoubted struggle that childhood involves. The primary school provides one environment where this struggle can be conducted in safety; certainly physical safety but psychological safety, too, if we are very lucky. One of the vital questions for teachers of our youngest children is how to develop the capacity to trust the natural inclination of the child and its inborn tendency to reach out to learn and to grow.

As well as great opportunities, there are also considerable dangers in designing schooling for this age group. Among the challenging educational issues facing our society in the future are:

1 How to avoid underestimating the innate capacity of the learner to reach out into the world.
2 How to avoid overestimating the need to fill children with information beyond their immediate needs, mistaking knowledge for understanding.
3 How to avoid viewing the pupil–teacher relationship as one of inequality, leading to excessive control over the process of learning.
4 How to avoid seeing the curriculum only in terms of content and recipes for knowing.
5 How to ensure that we take sufficient interest in pupils' own experience of life, developing a deep sensitivity to the struggles involved in managing it.

In primary schools, children are ambitious for themselves and optimistic for their futures. Cynicism has not yet been caught. The enormous task for the primary school teacher is to keep this true source of development and growth alive. Primary schools are essentially optimistic places with a concern for fulfilment, and primary school teachers are enormously ambitious for their pupils, investing heavily in their future success and happiness.

COHESION AND INTEGRATION

Post-modernism

The confusions and complexities of the current age have spawned the concept of 'post-modernism' to describe the ways in which the human management of the planet will have to change. In particular, it contests traditional assumptions and orthodoxies about the underlying purposes of human life and the ways in which human affairs are managed. Rather than continue to follow directions into the future laid down in the past for different times, progress towards a more sustainable future may lie in different and sometimes apparently contradictory directions. The promises about the future, extended by politicians, economists and scientists, have tended to rely on ideas such as the continual domination of nature, the centrality of reason in human affairs and increasing equity across the globe. This paradigm has fostered the rise of the nation-state, a capitalist economic world order, industrialism, bureaucracy, the dominance of secular values and the separation of private affairs from public ones. Above all, it has extended the belief that continually increasing economic prosperity is the only key to human achievement and happiness.

The last twenty-five years have seen the traditional classification of knowledge severely tested. New categories have been defined to cope with an ever increasing expansion in detail, and the inevitable building of relationships between the different subcategories of knowledge. Such reductionism has been regarded as necessary if we are to finally reveal the secrets of life and the universe. But there has also been a counter-trend, building new alliances of ideas and attempting to forge a new synthesis between classifications which have traditionally regarded themselves as antithetical – science and religion, economics and self-sufficiency, continuous depletion of raw materials and sustainability. In a recent book, Kevin Kelly (1994: 2) suggests a new alliance between living systems and machines will come to dominate development in the years ahead: 'The realm of the *born* – all that is nature – and the realm of the *made* – all that is humanly constructed – are becoming one. Machines are becoming biological and the biological is becoming engineered'.

The journey towards modernism has been guided by some major imperatives, what post-modernists call 'meta-narratives'. These meta-narratives prescribe the conditions necessary if humanity is to progress. One such meta-narrative suggests that the best way to understand life is to place organic, material and abstract phenomena in distinct categories, and develop different and separate theories about them. Schools have long accepted the curriculum as one such classification. The 1988 Education Reform Act was itself an act of modernism, extending by reinforcement the belief that continuing what we have always done in schools is the best way to prepare for a future that will be fundamentally different from the past.

Primary school educators have been instinctive post-modernists for over half a century. They have been highly sceptical about simple solutions to complex problems (e.g. the National Curriculum and testing), because they are so familiar with the nature of complexity in their working lives. Primary school teachers have not rejected the meta-narrative of the National Curriculum, but have refused to accept it as the sole and wisest framework upon which to develop an appropriate pedagogy for the twenty-first century. At the heart of the primary school approach to human growth, learning and development are the ideas of wholeness as opposed to fragmentation and of integration as opposed to separation. Primary schools have been significantly successful in achieving an appropriate blend of these apparent opposites, recognizing that success lies not in deciding on an 'either/or' basis, but proceeding with both as appropriate and necessary in the circumstances.

The term 'holistic' has entered the language to promote a view that an attention to wholeness is as important as attention to the separate and contributory parts. Deriving from the Greek *holos* (i.e. whole), the concept refers to an understanding of reality in terms of integrated wholes whose properties cannot be reduced to those of smaller units. The cognitive tyranny in education has produced a hierarchy of human attributes, placing intellectual rigour and physical prowess above emotion and intuition at the pinnacle of human expression.

Integration and connection

There are signs that reductionism is being challenged. New integrative and holistic theories can be seen coming together from work in the sciences, ecology, philosophy, health, therapy, sociology, religion and politics. A concern for connecting principles is emerging. This concern stresses the interdependence of every aspect of our environment. It suggests that descriptions of reality which focus on division and separation do not reflect with accuracy the way the world is and how we experience it. Rather, it extends the notion that we are all part of one interconnected and seamless planetary system. The scientist David Bohm (1980) coined the phrase 'the implicate order' to describe a view of the world in which consciousness and physical matter are part of an ever-changing flow. Existence is seen as a dynamic web of relationships, an unbroken wholeness in which every part unfolds and implicates every other. The theoretical scientist Fritjof Capra (1983) has suggested that the mechanistic world view of Newton and Descartes has brought us perilously close to destruction, and advocates a new vision, systems-based and holistic, which is more consistent with the findings of modern physics:

> This theory of integration and wholeness stands in contrast to the traditional theory of reductionism which demonstrates a preoccupation with seeking explanations to phenomena through fragmentation into smaller and smaller constituent parts. Human activity, like traditional scientific theorising, is characterised by division and distinction. Human endeavour is circumscribed within concepts of nationhood, language, religion, race, gender, class and economic wherewithal. We are labelled and compartmentalised according to such criteria and, in order to protect our interests, we learn to be secretive, devious and manipulative. We frequently come to regard others, especially those who are in different circumstances, as enemies to be feared, resisted, shunned, discriminated against, and in extreme situations, to be fought against and killed. What is worse, we have come to believe that these behaviours are both inevitable and acceptable and so we teach them to our children.
>
> (Capra 1983: 286)

Primary schools are engaged in a constant struggle to reconcile the need for separation with the need for integration. The attempt to establish curricula and pedagogies which achieve cohesion is a constant one. It is perhaps beyond possibility to capture it in guidelines and plans, since it exists as praxis – the continual interplay between what we do and how we experience it. Moments in classroom life are the developmental ore from which tangible insights and understandings are forged. The crucible is the learning activity and all that it involves in the heat of the moment, not the curriculum statement nor the development plan.

COMMUNITY

There is a commonly held assumption that education is a preparation for life. This raises some interesting issues such as when does life actually begin? Does a life-long learner actually have no life at all? This idea that somehow the act of preparation is not living – is not to be experienced as an intellectual, emotional and intuitive struggle with the world, its ideas and behaviours – is significant. Because if schooling is not life, then what is it? It is perhaps only when educators see learning as one of the central dynamics of life and living that its possibilities and potential truly begin to be understood. If we are transmitting to pupils the idea that at some, as yet, unspecified date in the future all the concepts and ideas vital to human health and happiness will simply click into place, then we are denying them responsibility for the development of their own lives.

Good primary education has challenged this assumption and attempted to provide an environment in which both the needs of the future and the needs of the present are catered for. What successful primary schools have always been good at, is creating conditions for a rich life within the school by reducing the overarching weight of institution and bureaucracy. It is very easy for pupils to pick up the idea that their role in the school is to serve the institution's purposes through obedience and correct behaviour, than to engage in a voyage of discovery during which the options and possibilities of their life are gradually unfolded.

In recent years, many schools have seen a development beyond institution, to the idea of community. The concept of community education enjoyed a spectacular peak during the mid-1980s, until the 1988 Education Reform Act brought schools back into bureaucratic line. Many schools and local education authorities had set in motion development projects and programmes to build into the education service a more substantial element of community. This had a number of focus points. First, there were the practical considerations: the under-utilization of educational facilities, the idea of the school as a more substantial resource for the neighbourhood, and the greater involvement of the local community in the life and work of its educational institutions. Secondly, there was the philosophical element, which included concepts of life-long learning and the provision of facilities and support beyond the limits of state-funded schooling. It encompassed the need to harness the personal and collective potential of people in communities, so that they could learn to take action to affect their lives, strengthening involvement in decision-making and reducing dependence on official structures.

In many situations, activity to deal with the practical aspects of community education preceded a thinking-through of the philosophical implications, and community education became a bolt-on addition to services rather than a fundamentally new way of handling the whole enterprise. Because it grew out of a political imperative, it tended to ignore the significant developments that had been taking place in primary schools over many years. Starting as a move away from the need to keep parents distant from the school, it grew into a movement towards greater parental influence in the life of the school and more profound relationships between the three key participants in the learning process – the learners themselves, their parents and their teachers in the school. The idea of partnership evolved, taking participation beyond the fund-raising focus that parent–teacher associations had often seen as their basic purpose.

The philosophical approach to community that focuses on the ethos and culture of participation has perhaps received less attention. This idea suggests that a sense of community is achieved when participants in an enterprise can develop involvement that goes beyond the superficialities of role and responsibility. It opens up the possibility of deeper and more profound communication and the development of high levels of trust and collaboration. Such a state is not easy to achieve, but primary schools have been one form of organization in our society in which the idea has been pursued with some vigour. Children will learn to be responsible citizens, good neighbours and committed friends if they are educated in an environment where the politics are consistent with the philosophy. It is no use claiming to be a caring community in the school brochure, and then engaging in behaviours which treat children's psychological needs with indifference. Primary schools have struggled to develop a community ethos, seeing their task as more than simply the provision of instruction but as a way of managing collective living within the physical and psychological boundaries of the school. Successful community is built on shared endeavour, trust and understanding. These are qualities that have been dismissed by some in recent years as unnecessary luxuries. They are basic to the process of growth, development and learning. To ignore them is to run the risk of seriously denying children their birthright. Schools are communities, and they have to be encouraged to build the sort of community spirit and ethos that will add so much to the quality of life as well as to the effectiveness of learning.

Primary schools are far more significant organizations than we have traditionally assumed. Their familiarity, and their focus on our youngest learners, have belied their essential complexity. They are a rich source of both inspiration and information about the challenges of developing organizational life in a high-pressure, confusing and fast changing world.

◆4◆ LEARNING AND TEACHING

Learning is what schools are about. The reason we need them is to create for children an appropriate environment in which the awesome process of learning about life, living and the world around them can be deliberately guided and encouraged. As the expectations on our schools increase, it will become ever more important to place the learning process itself right at the top of the agenda for our own professional learning and development.

Perhaps what we need first is a new focus for our considerations of learning and teaching. David Orr (1992) comments:

> Education in the modern world was designed to further the conquest of nature and the industrialisation of the planet. It tended to produce unbalanced, underdimensioned people tailored to fit the modern economy. Postmodern education must have a different agenda, one designed to heal, connect, liberate, empower, create and celebrate. Postmodern education must be life centred.

Orr is emphasizing the necessity of the paradigm shift examined in Chapter 2. He contrasts an approach to education based on scientific rationality, appearance and behaviour with another based on humanity, essence and experience. When we place life at the centre of our educational concerns, we see learning as a natural part of growth and development. This starting point recognizes that we are all born with an awesome potential for learning, and that education is the process of optimizing this precious resource. It places new emphasis on the importance of personal discovery as a key ingredient in the learning process, and values the emergence of a sense of wonder and mystery. At the same time, such an approach honours traditional virtues of respect for discipline and competence.

By focusing on the learner rather than the curriculum as the central foundation of schooling, we recognize the creation of a suitable climate and environment for learning as the key task. By encouraging the development of self-responsibility for learning, the humanistic approach strives to reduce pupil dependence on the teacher for direction, control, motivation and evaluation. It sees learning as an act of creativity, a bringing to life of human potential. Teachers have a significant role in safeguarding that potential, of creating conditions in which it can flourish and grow.

Eric and Carol Hall (1988: 15) link the development of the humanistic paradigm with the development of humanistic psychology, and offer a number of defining factors:

- In humanistic education learners are seen as having choices and cannot be limited by their heredity or past experience.
- Humanistic education is concerned with the whole person and places equal emphasis on the intellect and the emotions.
- Humanistic education aims for the full development of the individual.

Our education and upbringing has tended to emphasize the knowing dimension at the expense of the being, so that we can often arrive at the threshold of adulthood incomplete, and in many ways insufficiently equipped for the challenges and demands ahead. What is required is a balancing of the two, an integrating of what we know and what we are as a result of experience. This is not to suggest that knowing is of no importance, but to point to the dangers of relentlessly pursuing it to the exclusion of other important aspects of living and being. Our success as teachers depends upon our ability to help learners to break through the boundaries of self-limitation. This involves encouraging them to take risks with their learning, to bring out what is sometimes hesitant, raw and unrefined.

DEFINING THE TASK

Traditionally, learning has been seen as something that others do to us, rather than as something we do for ourselves. Many definitions of learning point to a process of acquisition – the child as an empty repository dependent on inputs from the adult world, gradually filling up during the processes of socialization and schooling. Success is measured in terms of how quickly and how completely this filling-up process is completed. Some new definitions and understandings are needed if we are to succeed in liberating learning from the stranglehold of traditional orthodoxies and the limitations of too narrow an understanding of its complex processes (Whitaker 1995).

When Plutarch observed that a child's mind is not a vessel to be filled but a fire to be kindled, he was setting a standard for life-centred definitions of learning. Others which are worthy of consideration include:

What a dangerous activity teaching is. All this plastering on of foreign stuff. Why plaster on at all when there is so much inside already.

(Ashton-Warner 1980: 14)

Learning should be a living process of awakening – a series of creative steps in unfoldment.

(Whitmore 1986: 11)

. . . releasing oneself, heart and soul into the world . . . developing the courage to push against boundaries and test new behaviours.

(Zinker 1977: 17)

The means by which people come to perceive, interpret, criticise and transform the worlds in which they live.

(Mezzirow 1983: 128)

One of the keys to understanding the learning process, and of being able to contribute to it successfully as an educator, is the appreciation that all the resources for learning are already within us, and are not acquired through teaching. Theodore Roszak (1981: 196) emphasizes the central importance of this potential:

We all bring into school a wholly unexplored, radically unpredictable identity. To educate is to unfold that identity – to unfold it with the utmost delicacy, recognizing that it is the most precious resource of our species, the true wealth of the human nation.

Good teaching can awaken and direct this potential, while at the same time encouraging and supporting the unfolding of identity and destiny. We need to appreciate that virtually all of us are born as 'going concerns', with all the resources for successful growth and development available to us at birth. Successful learners are those who are able to activate those resources in relation to circumstance and need.

Violet Oaklander (1978: 324) captures the wealth of these resources and many of the essential qualities of learning that children bring with them to school:

Children are our finest teachers. They already know how to grow, how to develop, how to learn, how to expand and discover, how to feel, laugh and cry and get mad, what is right for them and what is not right for them, what they need. They already know how to love and be joyful and live life to its fullest, to work and to be strong and full of energy. All they need is the space to do it.

In her study of children's thinking, Margaret Donaldson (1978: 111) concludes: '. . . there exists a fundamental human urge to make sense of the world and bring it under deliberate control'.

Perhaps more than anything, learning is a creative process, a bringing into being. Joseph Zinker (1977: 3–4) expresses something of its enormous complexity and tantalizing intricacy:

Creativity is a celebration of one's grandeur, one's sense of making anything possible. Creativity is a celebration of life – my celebration of life. It is a bold statement: I am here! I love life! I love me! I can be anything! I can do anything!

Creativity is not merely the conception, but the act itself, the fruition of that which is urgent, which demands to be stated.

Creativity is an act of bravery. It states: I am willing to risk ridicule and failure so that I can experience this day with newness and freshness. The person who dares to create, to break boundaries, not only partakes of a miracle, but also comes to realise that in the process of being . . . is a miracle.

LIFE-FOCUSED LEARNING

In attempting to create a conceptual framework for a more life-centred approach to learning, a number of factors need to be highlighted (Whitaker 1995: 7):

- *Personality*: how children acquire a self concept which reflects their successful experience as learners, both in the years before school and throughout their careers in formal education;
- *Aspiration*: how pupils are encouraged to define and pursue their own learning ambitions and to incorporate them comfortably within the curriculum framework of the school;
- *Needs*: how the emotional and psychological nourishment so vital to supporting the inherent potential to learn can be supplied within schools and classrooms;
- *Relationships*: how pupils can work together to develop the skills and qualities necessary to becoming successful learners, and how pupils and teachers can build creative mentoring partnerships to ensure sustained educational growth and development;
- *Interactions*: how pupils can be guided to use dialogue with their friends and teachers to explore and examine the challenges of the learning experience and so develop a sharp awareness of their own developing skills and abilities;
- *Values*: how pupils can be helped to develop a strong, satisfying and lasting relationship with learning and come to value the place of education in their lives;
- *Behaviour*: how pupils can be supported in becoming increasingly able to

take responsibility for the choices they make, the actions they pursue and the consequences they encounter;
- *Experience*: how pupils can be presented with opportunities to reflect on their experience of learning in order to make sense of it and so make considered choices about learning behaviour in the future.

These elements contribute in significant ways to the creation of satisfactory conditions for learning and teaching, and to the capacity of pupils to acquire and develop knowledge, skills and qualities in the collective setting of the classroom.

A life-centred approach to education places learning within the context of whole experience, rather than as only a part of experience. The traditional orthodoxies of education derive from a reductionist view of learning that emphasizes the processes of thinking and knowing at the expense of other aspects of human endeavour. The National Curriculum has been designed to give the strongest emphasis to knowledge. Attainment Targets currently give only grudging recognition to the non-cognitive aspects of learning.

In primary schools, we need to continue to strive to restore an appropriate balance to the learning process by giving the same high status to experience, imagination, creativity and intuition as we do to knowing, thinking, remembering and reasoning. As well as knowing about the world, we need to have the skills and qualities that will enable us to operate effectively in it. This will involve a reconsideration of both the curriculum we offer to pupils and the nature of the learning experiences that deliver it.

It is important to consider the different dimensions of personhood we bring to our growth and development. The psychologist Carl Jung (1971) has suggested that human completeness consists of four key attributes: the physical, the emotional, the intellectual and the intuitive. It is significant to note how in society and its education system, these attributes have been separated (see Fig. 4.1).

The vertical axis in Fig. 4.1 has been the obsession of the English public school for centuries. The horizontal axis – emotion and intuition – has been acknowledged, but disparagingly. Part of the public school ethic has been to develop character by concealing emotions and feelings and discouraging intuitive thinking and imagination. Only the virtues of rationality, logic and deductive thinking have been extolled. It is no coincidence that the polarization of these attributes has been a central feature of gender socialization. What are needed in our classrooms are opportunities to redress this harmful polarization. Emotional and intuitive development are vital if creativity is to be cultivated, and a more complete potential for growth and development released.

There has been a strong tendency in our society to prize the intellectual

Intellectual
How we develop, manage and communicate our
thinking, ideas, arguments, analysis and rationality.

Emotional		**Intuitive**
How we develop, manage		How we develop, manage and
and communicate our		communicate our hunches,
emotions and feelings.		gut reactions and insights.

Physical
How we develop and manage our
physical behaviour and communicate
through non-verbal signals.

Figure 4.1 Dimensions of personhood and learning.

dimension above the the emotional and intuitive and to denigrate and
disparage those who introduce feelings and intuitions into organizational
affairs. Bureaucracies are designed to operate according to rational principles, not to be sensitive to human needs and aspirations. Gender perceptions in particular have polarized in this way, creating a dangerous
incompleteness in the ways communication is regarded, both in personal
relationships and more especially in organizational life.

Effective learners are more likely to be those individuals who bring all
dimensions of being into the process of growth and development, thereby
increasing their capacity to draw upon a full range of qualities and skills.
For too long, the emotional and intuitive elements have been discounted
in organizational learning, inhibiting the full expression of human potential. When people are only operating on two of their available cylinders,
then serious underperformance is the inevitable result.

It is in the field of intelligence that new definitions and understandings
are particularly necessary. In its basic sense, intelligence is that property
which provides the potential for fulfilment in all aspects of our lives. It
provides the capacity for physical survival, emotional balance and intellectual enquiry. In the formal world of organized education, intelligence
has acquired a very restricted meaning – the ability to perform in a narrow range of cognitive activities. In these terms, our capacity to solve a
number puzzle is regarded as a sign of intelligence, whereas a capacity
to provide comfort and support to a friend in need, or to cook a nutri-
tious and tasty meal, is not.

At Harvard University, Howard Gardner (1993) has devised the concept of 'multiple intelligences' to describe an altogether enhanced view
of human intelligence, and is currently involved in co-directing Project
Zero, an investigation into the educational implications of this new concept. He suggests that there are seven basic intelligences:

- linguistic intelligence;
- logical/mathematical intelligence;
- spatial intelligence;
- musical intelligence;
- bodily/kinaesthetic intelligence;
- interpersonal intelligence;
- intrapersonal intelligence.

This alternative vision, he suggests, offers a radically different view of the mind: '. . . a pluralistic view which recognises many different and discrete facets of cognition, acknowledging that people have different cognitive strengths and contrasting cognitive styles' (Gardner 1993: 6).

This is very good news, because primary schools have been struggling for decades to move beyond a life-restricting definition of intelligence which has driven the learning process into tighter and tighter corners. The seven intelligences listed above are very much the curriculum which primary schools have been concerned with. Teachers in primary schools have a deep sense, that without this broader definition, their work in schools will be significantly undernourishing, sending children towards adult life without many of the basic ingredients for successful and happy living.

Gardner stresses that those involved in the direction of schooling systems need to embrace this new definition, and recognize in particular the limits to a narrow and monolithic approach to learning in schools:

> We are all so different largely because we all have different combinations of intelligences. If we recognise this, I think we will have at least a better chance of dealing appropriately with the many problems we face in the world. If we can mobilize the spectrum of human abilities, not only will people feel better about themselves and more competent; it is even possible that they will also feel more engaged and better able to join the rest of the world community in working for the broader good.
>
> (Gardner 1993: 12)

Perhaps one of the most frustrating challenges is that while we can isolate many of the elements that contribute to effective and successful learning, and point to some of the problems and difficulties that inhibit and frustrate it, the learning process itself is largely unpredictable, confusing, haphazard and messy. Perhaps what we need to learn more than anything else, is to trust the learners to do more of it for themselves. It is worth recalling the observations about good learners made by Neil Postman and Charles Weingartner (1971: 41–2):

- they enjoy solving problems;
- they know what is relevant for their survival;

- they rely on their own judgement;
- they are not afraid of being wrong and can change their minds when necessary;
- they are not fast answerers – they think first;
- they are flexible and adapt according to situation and challenge;
- they have a high degree of respect for facts;
- they are skilled in enquiry;
- they do not need to have an absolute, final, irrevocable solution to every problem;
- they do not get depressed by the prospect of saying *I don't know.*

As teachers, we need to be guided by the learners themselves. We have to create opportunities for them to talk about themselves as learners, about what excites them, frustrates them, challenges them and inspires them in their learning. We need to recognize that our single most important contribution to their future well-being is to help them to develop into effective and capable learners. Regarding the new educational challenges created by fast and accelerating change, Alvin Toffler (1971) notes that pupils will need skills in three crucial areas. First, they will need skills in learning itself. Schools must not only present data and information but help pupils to develop the skills of handling it. Pupils must learn how to discard old ideas and how to replace them. Secondly, they must learn about relating to others. Increasing pressures in society and faster change will increase the difficulties in maintaining human ties. Education must help pupils to accept the absence of deep friendships, to accept loneliness and mistrust, or it must find new ways to accelerate friendship formation. Thirdly, rapid change will multiply the kinds and complexities of decision-making facing individuals; therefore, education must address the issue of overchoice directly.

THE SKILLS OF TEACHING

Just as it is important to revise our definitions of learning and seek to develop a more life-centred understanding of a very complex process, so it is necessary to submit to re-examination our concepts of teaching and managing classroom life. One of the ways we can help to bring about a more informed approach to educational decision-making is to articulate a more comprehensive analysis of the work that teachers actually do. The current perception of teaching is dangerously limiting. Even in some initial training institutions, teaching is still regarded only as pedagogy – the science of teaching children. Very little attention seems to be given to the fact that in addition to a wealth of cognitive and curriculum considerations, teaching also encompasses a whole range of organizational issues that are generated when purposeful activity is conducted in a collective setting. Issues of institutional management, organizational psychology, culture, climate and personal welfare are major concerns for classroom teachers, demanding knowledge, skills and qualities beyond those traditionally associated with pedagogy. It is time that teachers in schools were afforded the same respect, understanding and training as those who occupy positions as managers in business organizations.

If we adopt the frequently used definition of management as getting things done with and through other people, we can see the relevance. Teachers are charged with tasks to do with organizing learning in a pupil community. The complexities of this responsibility are certainly equal to those experienced by senior managers in industrial and commercial organizations. But we still conceive of teaching as a discrete, specialized activity, somehow devoid of organizational and management implications. Educational management has tended to focus only on the non-educational elements of organizational life, and has concerned itself largely with the roles and responsibilities of senior staff. The essence of management in schools is the transaction of classroom learning. The coordination of a subject or department, while challenging and complex, is less significant by comparison. Perhaps the key contribution that management training and development can make to education, is to focus on the complexities of classroom life and the challenges to teachers of managing learning in a large group of pupils with different abilities, needs and behaviours.

One way to create a more complete understanding of teaching as managing is to examine the range of skills and qualities required to manage the process of learning effectively (Whitaker 1995). These fall into four distinct but related groups: (1) occupational, (2) personal, (3) managerial and (4) aspirational.

Occupational skills

These are the skills and qualities that are developed through training and experience. They are of a specialist and technical nature and specific to particular occupations and professions. Teachers have different occupational skills from nurses, lawyers or engineers, for example. In the teaching profession these may include:

- subject specialization;
- teaching methods and techniques;
- child development and psychology;
- history of education;
- curriculum design.

They are often the key focus of job-related training within organizations.

Personal skills

These are the skills and qualities acquired and developed through the process of socialization. Their purpose is to develop and sustain relationships and enable social living. They determine our capacity to get on well with other people in both professional and social settings. A complete list of personal skills and qualities would be very long indeed but would include:

- being courteous and considerate;
- conveying a sense of warmth;
- listening to what others say;
- speaking clearly and appropriately;
- being assertive;
- responding to the needs of others.

Until fairly recently, these skills rarely featured in the formal educational process, although they are constantly referred to by adults in the socializing of the young. While they are crucially important in teaching, they have rarely been the subject of training and development. It is often our relationships with others that cause our most difficult and emotionally painful moments. It is not surprising, then, that the additional pressures created in our work can increase challenge and stress in our own relationships.

Success in teaching requires us not only to be aware of this, but to improve our own skills in order to manage our relationships with others as effectively and sensitively as possible.

Managerial skills

These are the skills and qualities needed to work with and through other people. Teaching has not traditionally been associated with that professional activity known as 'management', but even a cursory glance at the following analysis will demonstrate that teaching is indeed a management activity *par excellence*. The following classification of managerial skills provides a useful starting point for consideration (Whitaker 1983):

Creating:
- having good ideas;
- finding original solutions to common problems;
- anticipating the consequences of decisions and actions;
- employing lateral thinking;
- using imagination and intuition.

Planning:
• relating present to future needs;
• recognizing what is important and what is merely urgent;
• anticipating future trends;
• analysing.

Communicating:
• understanding people;
• listening;
• explaining;
• written communication;
• getting others to talk;
• tact;
• tolerance of others' mistakes;
• giving thanks and encouragement;
• keeping everyone informed;
• using information technology.

Motivating:
• inspiring others;
• providing realistic challenges;
• helping others to set goals and targets;
• helping others to value their own contributions and achievements.

Organizing:
• making fair demands on others;
• making rapid decisions;
• being in front when it counts;
• staying calm when the going is difficult;
• recognizing when the job is done.

Evaluating:
• comparing outcomes with intentions;
• self-evaluation;
• helping to appraise the work of others;
• taking corrective action where necessary.

Aspirational skills

One of the most significant aspects of teaching work relates to the constant need to look ahead and to focus on the immediate as well as distant futures of children's lives. Learning is about constant and continual change. It involves a demanding regime of reaching beyond known limits and steadily enlarging repertoires of knowledge, understanding, skills, values, beliefs, competences and qualities. This requires of teachers enormous optimism, sensitive patience and unflagging belief in the process. More specifically, it requires a set of skills that keep a committed sense of striving and discovery at the forefront of classroom work. Among these aspirational skills and qualities are:

- activating potential;
- defining intentions;
- nourishing curiosity;
- expanding horizons;
- encouraging risk;
- supporting action;
- inspiring ambition.

Together these skills can combine to help pupils to develop self-belief in their capacities as learners, and assist in awakening a sense of ambitious possibility. It is when children begin to sense the power of their own potential, and are encouraged to experiment with it in a supportive climate, that learning becomes self-generating and deeply satisfying.

OPERATIONAL MODES

One of the most frustrating aspects of management work is realizing at the end of the day that although you have been exceedingly busy, many planned tasks and activities remain neglected and unattended to. Recently, time management has become something of a preoccupation as we struggle to pack more and more into the same amount of time.

Part of the desperation about time and workload arises out of a basic misperception about the nature of managerial work. Most of us see our roles as requiring us to attend to those tasks and activities designated in our job descriptions. We make plans and organize out time to deal with these requirements. What we find, however, as we set out to conduct these tasks, is that we are constantly interrupted. During the course of most days we find ourselves engaged in a series of interactions, few of which had been planned. People approach us and make requests. Often these approaches seem friendly and undemanding, prefaced by such phrases as 'Can I have a word?', 'Have you got a minute?' or 'Are you busy?'. The modesty of these requests usually belie their importance. Few of us turn down these requests; in fact, we tend to respond to them with willingness and sensitivity.

Taken individually, these interactions are usually very brief, seldom

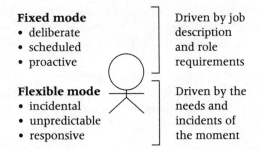

Fixed mode
- deliberate
- scheduled
- proactive

Driven by job
description
and role
requirements

Flexible mode
- incidental
- unpredictable
- responsive

Driven by the
needs and
incidents of
the moment

Figure 4.2   Operational modes.

longer than three or four minutes and often very much less, but they do create a diversion in our already tightly planned schedule. It is not uncommon to find that a succession of short interruptions has placed our whole schedule in jeopardy. The tendency is to blame ourselves for giving more attention to the apparently urgent, than to the important tasks we have set ourselves. We seem to find ourselves preoccupied with incidents and events that conspire to divert us from the real tasks and challenges of our roles. One of the consequences is that we can feel out of control, reacting to events rather than directing them. We can feel guilty because we are so driven by events and worried that perhaps we lack the skills for the job.

This presents a classic management dilemma. We have tended to think that good managers are always in control of their destiny and are only effective when they operate in a proactive way, demonstrating supreme control over their actions and the situations in which they find themselves. The reality is quite different. Far from dealing with trivia and apparently minor incidents, these interruptions are crucial to the well-being of the organization, enabling it to function effectively, to deal with its temporary difficulties and problems and to engage in the essential daily work. Research has shown (Mintzberg 1973) that management by interruption is a highly effective way of operating, creating countless opportunities for real issues to be dealt with, policies to be highlighted, values to be demonstrated and visions pursued. It is because managers are so good in this incidental mode that so many schools are well run, and are able to deal with their crises and satisfy the demands made of them.

Figure 4.2 suggests that teachers, like most managers, operate in two distinct but related modes: fixed and flexible. It is often in the flexible mode that managers do their most effective work. It is in the spontaneity of the moment that they are able to deal with the urgent issues, creatively helping others to gain the information they need, resolve their dilemmas and difficulties and receive the encouragement and reassurance that is so often necessary to function effectively.

One of the challenges of management work lies in placing these two modes in a realistic balance. Since the flexible mode tends not to be referred to in job descriptions, we do not afford it the importance it deserves, nor allocate time for it by not scheduling our deliberate work too tightly. We need to appreciate that being interrupted presents opportunities to lead and manage, to advance the work of the organization by responding to the needs of others, and by helping them to manage their work more effectively.

TEACHING AS LEADERSHIP

Another useful way to examine the nature of the teacher's role is through the concept of leadership. Teachers can be regarded as exercising one of the most demanding leadership challenges devised by society – the education of the next generation. Leadership can be regarded as that part of a manager's work concerned with helping people to tackle prescribed tasks to the optimum of their ability. It is concerned more with effectiveness than with efficiency, and more with quality than with attainment.

As well as considering leadership from the leader's own perspective, it is important to have regard for the needs that we have of our leaders. Good leaders seem have an infinite capacity not only to satisfy vital needs but also to anticipate them. Such a capacity grows out of four key qualities:

- genuine interpersonal behaviour;
- warmth, care and respect for those we work with;
- empathy;
- a strong and unshifting belief in the potential of others to grow, develop and change.

All of us are needy, and failure to get some very specific needs satisfied, particularly those that contribute to our pattern of motivation, can result in loss of confidence and enthusiasm; a sense of not being involved and a part of things; a feeling of being unappreciated and undervalued and a reduced sense of job commitment and energy. These are expensive losses which few organizations can afford. Good leadership is the delicate process of anticipating these needs in others and striving to satisfy them. This is as true for learners in classrooms as it is for workers in factories or offices. Teaching is an act of discovering what the felt needs of pupils are and the growth needs they invariably conceal. Figure 4.3 indicates a range of needs likely to be experienced quite frequently by pupils during the process of learning:

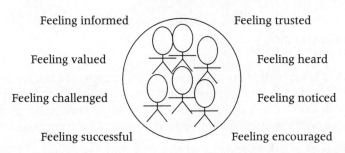

Figure 4.3 Leadership and needs.

Effective teachers are those who are able to reach out to pupils, to appreciate and understand their needs and seek specific and individual ways of satisfying them. Diana Whitmore (1986: 11) asserts: 'If children were to experience adults as welcoming, guiding and supportive, they would discover the wonder of life, the joy of exploring, the beauty of understanding'. As teachers we can help to create these felt experiences in pupils if we seize opportunities, usually in the flexible operational mode described above, to respond to some basic needs:

- *Trusting*: conveying to pupils a belief in their abilities. Resisting the temptation to increase control when things are difficult. Expressing delight at successes and achievements.
- *Listening*: constantly seeking opportunities to listen to pupils' current experiences. Asking questions, seeking information, eliciting opinions, delving into details and showing genuine interest and concern.
- *Noticing*: taking note of contributions and providing regular positive feedback on successes and achievements.
- *Encouraging*: empathizing with the demands and challenges of the learning process. Providing support for problem-solving and action-planning.
- *Developing*: offering practical help for those striving to make break-throughs in knowledge and skill. Working to create new learning opportunities and reinforcing success and achievement.
- *Challenging*: building a climate of systematic and continuous improvement. Constantly helping others to seek new angles, new possibilities and new ideas.
- *Valuing*: providing detailed and specific feedback so that all pupils feel a deep sense that their contributions and efforts are valued.
- *Informing*: keeping information flowing freely through the classroom. Checking that pupils know what is going on.
- *Supporting*: offering practical help as well as moral support. Getting

alongside pupils as often as possible. Providing a helping hand and a listening ear.

In the world of fast and accelerating change, the skills of effective leadership are developed in and through experience. Warren Bennis (1989: 146) notes:

> Leaders learn by leading and they learn best by leading in the face of obstacles. As weather shapes mountains, so problems make leaders. Difficult bosses, lack of vision in the executive suite, circumstances beyond their control, have been the leader's basic curriculum.

This suggests a radical revision of the way that leadership has traditionally been conceived. Teachers, like those in other leadership positions, must no longer assume they are where they are because of what they have learnt, but because they have a capacity to learn faster than the rate of change in the surrounding environment.

Eric Hoffer (1985) also emphasizes the importance of learning in the basic approach of effective leaders: 'In times of drastic change it is the learners who inherit the future, the learned find themselves equipped to live in a world that no longer exists'. This suggests a new vision of the pupil–teacher relationship, one that helps to destroy the idea that teaching is an elite and specialist occupation. Theodore Roszak (1981) suggests that in every educational exchange it is the teacher who must first learn something. In approaching pupils, there are vital questions to consider:

- Who is this child?
- What does he or she bring to this situation?
- What is there here for me to discover that no-one else has ever known before?

It is through interactions with pupils, what Roszak describes as 'glad encounters with the unexpected', that we can engage in discovering and empowering each child's learning destiny.

Teaching and leadership are both concerned with helping others to see that something is possible, and supporting them in the process of removing the blocks which prevent them standing on their own two feet. Daniel Rosenblatt (1975) described it as 'offering a kind of hope that change is possible'. Leadership, like teaching, creates an atmosphere that promotes the taking of small steps towards change, change that is free of shame, fear, guilt, humiliation and degradation:

> There has to be some kind of educational process bringing the art of living into day to day management. There has always been a complete difference between the way individuals relate to their colleagues and the way they relate to their friends and family. In the latter area,

kindness, tolerance etc, are not regarded as sentimental and wet, but as making the relationship work. Can one parallel this in business now? The difference between the two sets of attitudes is beginning to narrow and that may be the answer to tomorrow's problems.

(Kinsman 1990: 264)

This quotation highlights a key challenge for teachers and leaders: to counter the traditional and unnecessary separation in organizations of the personal and the professional. People are whole beings and are at their best when they feel complete and integrated. The separation into parts of ourselves is one of the most damaging tendencies in human activity.

There are no simple solutions in management because there are no simple problems. If problems were simple and straightforward there would be no need for management in the first place. Leadership is an active response to complexity, an ambitious striving towards achievement in awkward situations. It is a journey of belief and hope and downright determination.

It is in the classrooms of our primary schools that leadership and management of great dexterity and subtlety is practised. Unlike management structures in large business organizations, where the planning, organizing and evaluating are separated out to specialists in specific function departments, primary school teachers engage constantly and simultaneously in the whole gamut of management functions. Their work involves a complex intertwining of all the leadership and management skills that we regard as significant.

There is considerable new work to be done here. We need to create new insights and explanations of the intricate nature of management and leadership work in classrooms. As the future places ever new demands and higher expectations on schools and teachers, it will become increasingly important to have more complete models of professional practice to guide initial teacher education, and to help experienced teachers in the vital process of professional renewal and development.

5 CULTURE AND WELL-BEING

Visitors to British primary schools frequently comment on the fact that they are both comfortable and interesting places to be in. They observe the atmosphere of peaceful industry, and the commitment of both pupils and teachers to the tasks in hand. There is usually a great deal to look at. Primary schools are one of the few organizations which place a high priority in creating a visually stimulating environment, and one that is constantly changing. Some primary schools are a veritable feast of information, ideas, impressions and reflections. Good primary schools create a visual experience which both reflects the values at the heart of the organization and celebrates the work of its members.

Over the last half century, we have witnessed a transformation in the appearance of primary schools. From institutions of rigidity and regimentation, we have seen the learning environment develop into one which both respects and stimulates the learners who work in it. We have seen schools develop from places where movement away from desks was discouraged, to the free and purposeful movement that needs to accompany serious learning. Watching primary school children at their work is one of the most fascinating and instructive activities available to us. It is sad that so many people are so critically dismissive of the ways in which our youngest pupils go about their learning work. Comment is often made about how much time they spend off-task. Observation in local authority education departments, or even the Department of Education and Employment, will reveal constant distractions from task, casual conversations, wandering around, trips to lavatories and refreshment rooms. If this is the normal way that committed adults go about their business, why is it so wrong for children to do the same? Perhaps it is part of the belief that unless learning is unpleasant and painful, it cannot be effective. When we watch the attentiveness of young children to tasks they are both interested in and committed to, we note the power of their absorption and engagement, and their strong resistance to distraction.

Beyond the undoubted visible richness of good primary schools, there is something more elusive and intangible – an atmosphere of purposeful calm. Primary schools more than any other type of organization seem to achieve a happy balance between task and process – what has to be done with attention to the comfort and well-being of those involved. It is this which has changed so much over the last half century and is now in danger of being inhibited in its effective development. Sir Alec Clegg (1980) once remarked that it was not teaching style that made the difference to children's capacities to learn effectively, nor whether the school was traditional or progressive, but whether a love of learning was at the heart of what pupils and teachers did together. His worst possible scenario for a primary school was graphically described as being 'like a wet playtime all day'. The best primary schools are not soft and sentimental, nor are they rigid and regimented. They are ambitious places, and in seeking to fulfil their aspirations, they appreciate the vital importance of a sense of well-being in both pupils and teachers.

ORGANIZATIONAL CULTURES

Organizations, like families, are human systems in which a whole range of personal, social, psychological and political dramas are played out. Difficulties and challenges are created because it is not easy to achieve agreement about the script, the roles that people play and how the various acts and scenes are to be performed. In bureaucratic organizations there tends to be pressure to adhere to the script, but in other types of organization there is often more room for improvisation.

Culture refers to the ways in which the various participants in organizational life – the staff and their pupils – experience their day-to-day work, and the extent to which they feel able to commit themselves to the tasks and activities they are responsible for. While there is a great deal of theory about organizational cultures available to us, particularly from organizational psychologists and researchers into human potential and motivation, comparatively little of it seems to enter the curriculum of management training. An obsession with task, of getting vital jobs of work done efficiently and cheaply, means that the vital work of understanding the inner worlds of individuals, and the social conditions and dynamics under which they carry out their professional work, tends to be ignored.

When we become part of an organization, we find ourselves in two distinct types of environment. First, there is the physical environment, that which we experience with our senses. This includes the building, the fixtures and fittings, the furniture and all the material resources. It also includes the people who work there, what they say and what they do. This sensate environment can be observed and documented. It can be filmed and recorded, and it can be witnessed, both by its regular participants as well as by casual and occasional visitors. Secondly, there is the invisible, but equally significant, psychological environment, that which is experienced mentally and felt emotionally by those who work there. This environment is not available to observation, filming or recording. It consists of the internal constructs and meanings which each participant creates, and adapts, from moment to moment in the course of daily life in that organization. It is to this second environment that we need to give more attention, for it is here that many of the clues to human effectiveness, efficiency, enterprise and success are to be found.

Organizational cultures are ecologies within which the social, psychological and interpersonal dynamics of a group of people are worked out. Peter Anthony (1994: 31) suggests that: 'Cultures may provide the basic, theoretical and perceptual building processes upon which we rely to organize our inchoate experiences'.

The significant features of modern organizational cultures include:

• the richness of personal experience represented in them;
• the messiness of events and incidents;
• an uncertainty about tomorrow;
• disorder despite efforts at organizational tidiness;
• fun and enjoyment in daily life;
• enthusiasm and excitement;
• anguish and despair.

Given encouragement, people can make the best of most situations. The challenge for the future comes in taking the matter of culture more seriously than we have done so in the past, recognizing that quality and effectiveness depend very much on how people are feeling moment by moment during the school day, and how people who are expected to carry out the key work of the organization are treated. Figure 5.1 attempts to categorize the variables that affect life in an organization.

Cultural zones

Figure 5.1 outlines four specific clusters of factors. In reality there will be countless more, and reality can never be as simple as the diagram suggests. Most of us, when we think back through our experiences of organizational life in the home, at school and at work, are likely to respond through memory to the idea of psychological zones such as comfort zones, uncertainty zones, failure zones and confusion zones. In conversation about our organizational experiences, most of us can recall very specific memories, remembering the powerful emotions we were feeling, and sometimes the fine details of facial expression in those we were interacting with at the time.

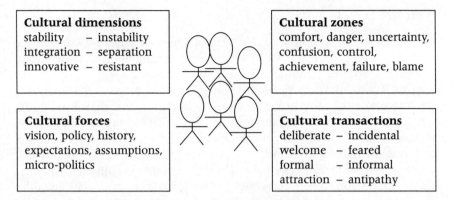

Cultural dimensions	Cultural zones
stability – instability integration – separation innovative – resistant	comfort, danger, uncertainty, confusion, control, achievement, failure, blame

Cultural forces	Cultural transactions
vision, policy, history, expectations, assumptions, micro-politics	deliberate – incidental welcome – feared formal – informal attraction – antipathy

Figure 5.1 Variable dynamics in organizational life.

In one sense, organizational life is all about zone travel. In the densely packed activity of organizational life, we move from one experience to another, each with its attendant issues, ideas, actions and reactions. To each we will react internally, sometimes with pleasure, sometimes with pain and occasionally with indifference. When we get home at the end of the day, it is not so much the events themselves we wish to review and reflect on, but the inner turmoils they have generated and the confusions and uncertainties they often create.

Cultural transactions

Organizations are sustained through interaction. In some kinds of work this increasingly involves relating to the hardware and software of information technology systems. But in more people-focused organizations like primary schools, interactions are the essence of work. Through them we discharge our responsibilities, create powerful relationships, offer information and receive feedback. Some interactions are planned, but many, perhaps the majority, are unexpected and incidental. We meet a colleague in a corridor and take the opportunity to transact some business. Sometimes a whole new course of events and incidents is set up on the basis of a chance encounter. Some interactions we welcome and look forward to.

In some relationships we feel at our best, perhaps being liked and respected by the other person. In other relationships we feel a sense of fear and dread rising within us as we make the journey to work in the morning. Some interactions are formal and conducted within a strict protocol of behaviour. Others are more informal and relaxed. We experience affection for some colleagues and respect their work. There are some we suspect dislike us, but we are never quite sure and they never actually say so. Organizational life is a long-running drama without a script.

Cultural forces

As we go about our daily life at school, most of us are aware of the powerful inner forces at work. While neither tangible nor visible, they exercise a relentless, sometimes insidious power over us. The history and traditions of an organization can sometimes be like this. It is as if there are a set of unwritten taboos to be observed and that if we transgress we will somehow upset not only the founding fathers, but everyone who has ever trodden there before us. In some organizations, the vision is everything and there is a powerful forward momentum which must not be hindered. The belief systems which we construct to guide us in our organizational behaviour are a vital part of our relationship to our work, and deeply affect how we go about performing our duties and responsibilities. This is the world of organizational politics, and the struggle to understand how power and authority are exercised and how we can best relate to them.

Cultural dimensions

Finally, Fig. 5.1 refers to more collective aspects where the organization can be considered as a whole – the participants as an organizational community. One of the disturbing trends in recent years has been increased instability, and many organizations find themselves in varying states of uncertainty and confusion. Then there is the dimension between integration, where everyone seems to be pulling together and there is a sense of shared endeavour, and separation, where everyone seems to be at cross-purposes. In these days of rapid change, another tension is the turbulence created by constant requirements for alteration and improvement. Leadership and management work is all about balancing these awkward and often unpredictable movements, and the effects they can have on the individuals concerned.

It is within this inner world that the secrets of organizational success and failure are to be found, and where we must look for the clues to why some people with apparently modest talents and abilities thrive in the organizational culture, whereas others with more spectacular skills and enterprise seem to fail the struggle.

SYNTROPIC AND ENTROPIC CULTURES

It is here that the work of biological scientists like Ilya Prigogine (1979) and Albert Szent-Gyoergyi (1974) on syntropy and entropy in organic systems provides a useful framework. They observed that some organic cultures have an enhancing or syntropic effect, tending to display increasing

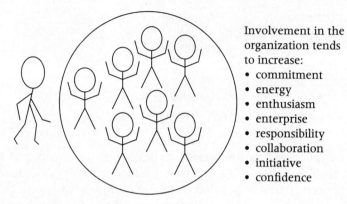

Involvement in the organization tends to increase:
- commitment
- energy
- enthusiasm
- enterprise
- responsibility
- collaboration
- initiative
- confidence

Figure 5.2 Syntropic culture.

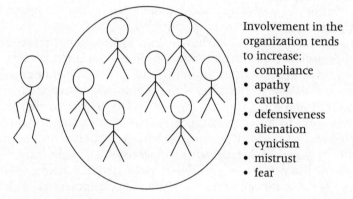

Involvement in the organization tends to increase:
- compliance
- apathy
- caution
- defensiveness
- alienation
- cynicism
- mistrust
- fear

Figure 5.3 Entropic culture.

energy, order and organization (see Fig. 5.2). Others have an inhibiting or entropic effect, tending towards disorder, deterioration and depletion of energy (Fig. 5.3). Translated to the workplace, these ideas provide us with a useful theoretical model.

In reality, no organization conforms to either of these extreme positions, but exists somewhere on the continuum between the two. Neither are the cultural forces ever static, but create movement in either direction through mood swings, bad days, calm periods and moments of crisis. The psychosocial landscapes of organizational cultures are the product of the human forces at work within them and include:

- power and authority structures;
- rules and regulations governing staff;
- attitudes of senior to junior staff;
- age profiles;

- status differentials;
- reward and punishment systems;
- patterns of rights and responsibilities;
- degrees of discrimination;
- management systems;
- celebration and acknowledgement of success;
- staff involvement in decision-making;
- access to information.

These factors create an important agenda for management and leadership work. The building of a syntropic culture is never easy. One of the most important tasks facing staff in primary schools is to work collaboratively to create management cultures which both enhance the strategic work of the school, but which also address the crucial issues of welfare and well-being of both staff and pupils.

Another useful way of approaching the management of organizational culture is to consider the more specific factors which create syntropy and cause entropy. Studies have shown that organizational behaviour and work performance are directly affected by the assumptions held about them by those in positions of authority and power. The enormous potential which staff and pupils bring with them to school every day tends to be activated and enhanced when senior staff believe in that potential and seek ways to foster its energetic release. This potential can also be thwarted and frustrated if senior staff believe that effective performance will only be achieved through strong supervision and tight control. When these assumptions are translated into management behaviour, then either they tend to operate like nutrients, enhancing the potential of others, or toxins, crushing and inhibiting that potential.

Cultural toxins

Among the many toxins that can act powerfully to inhibit our potential are those verbal and non-verbal behaviours which activate particular emotions such as fear, anger, resentment and jealousy. Such emotions can be stimulated when we are on the receiving end of particular types of communication behaviour:

- having our ideas rejected or stolen;
- facing constant, carping criticism;
- being ignored;
- being judged;
- being over-directed;
- not being listened to;
- being misunderstood.

Such behaviours occur all the time in most organizations, but when they are employed consistently and systematically, they can seriously undermine self-esteem, confidence, commitment and professional ambition.

Of particular significance are those behaviours which tend to arise out of a traditional preoccupation with sharply differentiated organizational hierarchies. When management behaviour reinforces status separation, then those lower down the hierarchical triangle can experience a range of painful and inhibiting feelings:

- a sense of inadequacy;
- inability to express oneself;
- inability to influence anyone;
- feelings of being shut out;
- increased cynicism;
- increased destructive feelings;
- feeling that one has either to dominate or be dominated;
- feeling that to conform is the best thing;
- feeling that intolerance and oppression have to be accepted;
- feeling that new ideas can only come from the top;
- feeling that there is no way to communicate with those at the top.

As long ago as 1960, in his pioneering work on organizational behaviour, Chris Argyris coined the phrase 'cultural pathologies' to describe such entropic characteristics as dependence, compliance, resistance, complacency, inhibition, depression and resentment. He claimed that when these were constantly present in the members of organizations, their potential to give of their best was significantly reduced.

Part of our organizational history has been the sustaining of a tradition that those who run organizations need to see the human spirit as their enemy, rather than as their most awesome ally. The psychologist David Smail (1987) notes the extent to which the exploitation of people has become endemic in organizations. He suggests that because so much of this exploitation is dishonourable, we hide its nature from ourselves. He urges a drastic shift in assumptions: 'Far from being repairable machines, human beings are embodied organisms on which damage will at least leave a scar. We simply cannot get away with using and abusing each other as we do' (Smail 1987: 3).

An index search through a collection of recent books on management and leadership found frequent references to such items as strategy, competitive edge, team-building, market forces, innovation, customer service, quality control and delegation. It is interesting to note there were no references at all, even in books with sections on organizational culture, to such items as community, justice, ethics, fear, oppression, happiness, fun, love or affection.

Cultural nutrients

Among the many nutrients that can act effectively to enhance our potential are those verbal and non-verbal behaviours which arouse positive and pleasurable emotions, such as excitement, joy, delight, happiness and affection. Such emotions can be stimulated when we are on the receiving end of particular types of communication behaviour:

- being valued;
- being encouraged;
- being noticed;
- being trusted;
- being listened to;
- being respected.

The essence of effective leadership is helping people to be as effective as they themselves would like to be. This involves supporting people to release their talents and abilities from self-restriction and encouraging them through positive attitudes and behaviours. Gerard Egan (1977) has highlighted the following stances towards others as being particularly nourishing:

- *Being 'for' others*: this involves showing an interest in others, sharing in their successes as well as their difficulties and being ready with support when it is needed.
- *Being attentive*: listening with care and attentiveness to the other person, being prepared to give time to them. It involves commenting on those things that others do that give us satisfaction and pleasure and offering support when things seem to be difficult.
- *Cooperation*: being prepared to work alongside others, to seek their support as well as to offer our own. It also involves showing enjoyment of other people's skills and contributions in collaborative ventures.
- *Regard for individuality*: accepting and valuing the fact that we are all different and that we tackle things in different ways. Not expecting others to be like us.
- *Regard for autonomy*: respecting that others know their own experience best and are capable of taking responsibility for themselves. Avoiding the tendency to dominate and control.
- *Assuming goodwill*: few people in organizations are consistently motivated by maliciousness. Most of us want to do our best and feel effective and valuable. Because we do not always like what other people do does not mean that they intended to upset us.
- *Understanding*: spending time with people, watching what they do and listening to what they say. Working to appreciate and understand their point of view.

- *Warmth*: being sensitive and considerate to others. Conveying a sense of caring about what other people are doing and how they feel.
- *Support and encouragement*: being aware of other people's needs and demonstrating a willingness to help them. Showing appreciation of what others do and an interest in the tasks they are currently engaged in.
- *Genuineness*: contrary to much of our socialization it is a major sign of respect to show yourself to others as you really are.

The art of building and maintaining an enhancing management culture for a primary school depends upon the style of leadership adopted by all of us who have management responsibilities. It is especially important that we see the major part of our role as working to satisfy the complex pattern of personal and professional needs colleagues bring with them to school every day.

Leadership thus becomes a process of interacting with colleagues in ways that help to satisfy their felt needs of the moment. Leadership is subtle work, and has developed radically in most schools from the command and control styles of earlier generations. Now it is not so much a case of who is a leader and who is not, but how each of us can effectively exercise that leadership aspect of our role and how we can offer leadership in a whole variety of situations. In this way, leadership becomes more than the exercising of status and position, it becomes a function of all those involved in the co-management of the school.

Those with specific leadership responsibilities are particularly well placed to communicate in ways that both enhance the capacity of colleagues to work effectively, and help to build a climate conducive to growth and development. Effective leadership is about supporting the vast resources for self-understanding, learning and growth within each other. These resources are more likely to be activated and released when a positive climate of psychological safety and support is created.

Cultural issues

Three particular issues lie at the heart of effective culture building: inclusion, affection and control. Each of these issues is crucially important as we work our way through the evolutionary crisis and will become increasingly significant as primary schools continue to break new ground into the future. Unless hard-pressed staff feel a powerful sense of belonging to the school and a feeling of involvement in its development, they are unlikely to feel sufficiently supported to give of their best. It is also important to recognize that while school effectiveness does not depend upon everyone liking each other, warmth and affection need to be part of organizational experience if trust is to be built and psychological security established. Constant attention to issues of control will be required if schools are to avoid ignoring crucial cultural dynamics and reinforcing the toxins that can be so destructive.

While good primary schools are particularly strong on affection and inclusion, there is often room for development in relation to the control issue. A tradition of strong leadership through the role of the headteacher has sometimes made it difficult for responsibilities to be spread throughout the whole staff. If we are to create more genuinely co-managing organizations, then the issue of control has to be confronted.

Charles Handy (1976) points to a strong relationship between the exercise of control and the amount of trust experienced by others. He illustrates this by suggesting that the sum of trust plus control is always constant. An increase in leader power and control causes a decrease in the subordinate's perception of trust:

$$\text{Control} + X = \text{trust} - X$$

But if the leader wants to increase trust, then it is necessary to relinquish some control:

$$\text{Trust} + Y = \text{control} - Y$$

Increasing trust is in the best interests of primary schools and is a vital factor in their future development. This will involve senior staff, heads in particular, in releasing control in areas such as decision-making, policy development, goal-setting and resource allocation. Headship needs to be seen as a function rather than a role, involving all members of the staff team. Headship will perhaps need to be reconceived as a collective, a collaborative venture drawing on a wider range of skills and qualities than have traditionally featured in the management process. Headteachers have their most important contribution to make in cultural leadership, giving attention to the issues outlined above, striving to create and maintain the best conditions in which the challenging processes of learning and teaching can best be conducted.

CULTURE AND CLASSROOM LIFE

One of the fascinating complexities of primary school life is the presence of three distinct but related cultural environments. First, there is the culture of the school as a whole, its pupils, teachers, parents and governors working together. Secondly, there is the management culture, the staff building the structures and processes through which the school can satisfy its purposes. Thirdly, there is an organizational culture within each individual class – pupils and a teacher working together in pursuit of learning objectives. While the principles discussed above are relevant to all three environments, the primary school classroom is a unique phenomenon in organizational studies and deserves specific attention.

Primary school teachers are unusual in starting their careers in charge of quite large organizations – a learning company of thirty or so individuals. In terms of the responsibilities and challenges this presents, they compare favourably with chief executives of medium-sized companies. Yet in many senses their task can be considered to be more challenging. They have little control over raw materials – primary schools tend to admit all-comers; they have the most elusive product of all – the inner process of mental and emotional change; they have to manage on an unbelievably small budget; and they have to satisfy the ambitious expectations of pupils and parents, the strictures of a somewhat superficial inspection system as well as society at large.

Creating an organizational culture conducive to effective learning in classrooms involves consideration of a range of factors:

- the age of the children;
- the process of growth;
- the nature of learning;
- emotional vulnerability;
- psychological security;
- physical safety;
- individuality;
- organizational life;
- life experience.

These factors feed into virtually all decisions that schools make about their pupils, and each plays a vital part in the ways that teachers manage the classroom process. The teachers have to know about all of them, they cannot specialize, and their art is essentially pragmatic and intuitive. Their knowledge and insight derives from experience and observation of the children they work with, yet little credit is ever given for the complexity and enormity of this process.

The prime responsibility for creating an effective classroom culture lies with the teacher, and much will depend upon the assumptions about pupils and their learning which have contributed to the forming of a particular teaching style. It is unfortunate that at a time when we are witnessing the fragmentation of family life, the disintegration of local communities and increasing social tension, that reforms to schooling emphasize the curriculum imperative and ignore the social dimension.

Central to the creation of a positive culture for learning is attention to the needs and interests of the learners themselves. It is not enough to claim that they are too young to know what is good for them, because by five most children have developed an acute awareness of interpersonal dangers, psychological violence and emotional pain. Writing of the need to involve pupils in the culture-building process, Jack Canfield and Harold Wells (1976: 6) observe:

> Students have a vested interest in the emotional environment of the classroom. Teachers and students should sit down together and freely discuss cooperation and competition, trust and fear, openness and deceit, and so on. These and many other topics discussed in classroom meetings help create the kind of climate that fosters total pupil growth.

Observation of primary school classrooms will reveal that a positive climate is created when teachers:

* enjoy relationships with their pupils;
* express their own needs and wishes to pupils;
* are understanding and accepting of pupils;
* foster and encourage warm and friendly relationships between pupils;
* spend more time listening to pupils than talking to them.

In specific terms, the classroom climate can be facilitated by maintaining interpersonal communication at a positive and caring level. Examples of this style of communicating are:

* Dealing with important interpersonal issues when and as they arise, not leaving them until later.
* Talking directly to pupils, rather than about them to the class as a whole.
* Speaking to pupils with courtesy, care and consideration.
* Being aware of the importance of eye contact and non-verbal communication.
* Avoiding the common blocks to effective communication, i.e. judging, criticizing, preaching, commanding and moralizing.

But there is much more to building an effective classroom culture than good communication. The future will demand that we continue to seek ways to help pupils to develop a whole range of skills and abilities not traditionally regarded as part of the curriculum for schools. Not only are these vital life skills that will be needed later in adult life, they are the very skills that will enable pupils to become more committed and responsible learners while they are at school. It is in the primary school classroom that this process should begin and it is vital that we develop a curriculum which includes attention to the following processes (Whitaker 1995):

* management skills;
* planning and goal-setting;
* choice and decision-making;

- cooperation and involvement;
- accountability.

Management skills

The word 'management' tends to be used to refer to a set of skills unique to people in high-status positions in organizations. Recently, a wider definition has emerged which regards management as a set of skills that enable us to tackle the challenges that face us in various aspects of our lives. Society has tended to sort us into those who manage and those who are managed, yet we serve in both capacities throughout our lives. What is important is that learners acquire sufficient management skills to give them the optimum capacity for self-management, self-direction and self-responsibility, and which will enable them to contribute creatively to the culture-building process.

One way of looking at the skills of management is to consider the elements of management referred to in Chapter 4: creating, planning, organizing, evaluating, communicating and motivating. There is much that we can do, even within the current curriculum framework, to help pupils to develop facility in these important areas. Children are natural managers and it is vital for the schooling system to build on these emerging capacities. Management training is something that should continue when children start school, not something undertaken as remedial work when adults get into supervising roles very much later in life. The following aspects of personal management should also feature in the curriculum:

- develop a sense of direction in life;
- build self-esteem and self-confidence;
- make life choices;
- develop personal skills and abilities;
- personal effectiveness;
- manage stress and crisis points.

Traditional views of childhood have tended to reinforce a somewhat limited and incomplete view of pupil potential and ability. Primary school children have demonstrated their capacity for rapid and complex learning through their association with modern information technology such as video-recorders and computers. In these fields, pupils often outskill their teachers. Developing enhanced management skills in the classroom is well within their grasp and should be regarded as a high priority.

In *The Personal Management Handbook*, John Mulligan (1988: 9) observes:

> In today's complex world, just surviving requires skilful personal management. Realizing your own potential, and helping to realize

that of others, demands highly sensitive and well developed personal management skills. Rounded development, including the ability to manage yourself and others, is not being formally recognized as a vital part of the manager's toolkit. And effective personal management is essential if you are to make the most of your life and potential, whether you are managing a large organization, your own life affairs or bringing up a family.

We must challenge the view that the traditional and formal curriculum of schools will equip learners adequately with the life management skills so necessary for self-fulfilment and happiness.

Planning and goal-setting

Planning is a key ingredient in getting things done effectively. This applies to learning in classrooms as much as to the activities of large organizations. The quality of learning can be improved considerably if pupils are given time and training in the skills of planning work.

Sadly, pupils are rarely given the opportunity in schools to identify and consider their own learning needs and hopes. The 1988 Education Reform Act has produced a seemingly endless flow of glossy brochures for parents and detailed folders of data for teachers, but nothing at all for the pupils themselves, explaining how these new educational phenomena are designed to affect their lives. There is still the remnant of a belief that, given a chance, pupils would choose inappropriate material for study or seek to avoid *work*. But responding to pupils' needs and hopes is much more than merely offering choices. Deep down most pupils want to succeed in those things that schools and society traditionally hold dear – the skills of literacy and numeracy. What we need to provide are chances for pupils to address the nature of their own learning, to take some responsibility for it, and to take risks in reaching out for what seems a bit beyond them without fear of failure.

We can begin to do this by exercising more skill in sensing our own pupils' frustrations and unsatisfied learning needs. Life-centred learning is really about being able to do this well. One positive and practical step is to help pupils develop proficiency in goal-setting. Far too often pupils embark on learning activities without knowing why they are doing them, how they will benefit, and in what form the final outcome will be assessed. We should always share the purposes and objectives of any learning activity we facilitate with our pupils. Pupils themselves should also be encouraged to be active in clarifying these aims for themselves. The approach outlined for the management of development projects in the next chapter can also be used successfully with pupils, helping them to improve significantly the capacity to manage their own learning.

Choice and decision-making

Effective learning is dominated by choosing and yet the processes involved in sensible and responsible decision-making have rarely featured in the curriculum. One of the purposes behind the move from a teacher- to a learner-centred model of education is the determination to reduce the sort of teacher-dependence characteristic of a schooling system based on instruction. The realization that learners are equipped with a huge capacity for learning, which is only likely to be harnessed if the right environment is created, has presented the need to help learners to accept and develop increasing responsibility for their own learning. This involves the skilful and responsible exercising of choice.

A useful concept to help our understanding of this process is that of the *locus of control*. Rotter (1966) suggests that it is possible to distinguish two particular control dynamics in human behaviour. The first of these labels those people who feel very much in charge of themselves and agents of their own destinies as 'internals' – their locus of control is within themselves. Those who feel they have very little control over what happens to them are labelled 'externals' – their locus of control is perceived as being outside themselves. J.E. Phares (1976) makes it very clear that those who operate with an internal dynamic are better able to make choices in their lives, take responsibility for their own actions and the consequences of them, and are better able to cope with failure and learn successfully from it. In particular, Phares discovered that internals:

- have greater self-control;
- are better at retaining information;
- ask more questions of people;
- notice more of what is happening around them;
- are less coercive when given power;
- see other people as being responsible for themselves;
- prefer those activities which require skill than those involving chance;
- have higher academic achievements;
- are more likely to delay gratification;
- accept more responsibility for their own behaviour;
- have more realistic reactions to their own successes and failures;
- are less anxious;
- exhibit less pathological behaviour.

Most of these outcomes would be on most teachers' list of desirable attributes in learners, yet for far too long the schooling system has been pursuing an approach to learning which reinforces an external dynamic – a belief that other people are responsible, and that only the teacher is in a position to make decisions about an individual pupil's learning.

The implications from this research are clear. When learners are able to accept responsibility and choice in their learning they are likely to be more successful. As teachers we need to cultivate an internal dynamic in our classrooms, and discourage that most limiting condition: teacher-dependence.

The journey to self-responsibility will not be achieved if we concentrate only on the content of the curriculum and not on the processes involved in being an effective learner. Everyday, pupils in classrooms exercise choices, select responses and make decisions. Unless they are very lucky, they are unlikely to have been taught what the specific ingredients of intelligent choosing or decision-making consist of. The educational system will never successfully assist the journey from dependence to independence without opportunities to acquire the skills that accompany successful self-management in a modern world.

Cooperation and involvement

Many of the skills that are selected as the basis for management training later in life (e.g. motivation, leadership, teamwork, planning and communication) are naturally present in young children and evident in their play. As the schooling system strengthens its grip of control, developing a competitive rather than cooperative and participative approach to learning, these skills fail to be built on and developed. Management training becomes a mid-life remedial exercise. By insisting that pupils learn individually and separately, we are failing to take advantage of one of the key opportunities provided in schools – a collaborative setting.

While competition tends to be promoted as the vital ingredient in schools, it is likely that the success of the human race will depend more on cooperation. Although conducted in the collective setting of the classroom, learning in schools has tended to focus on the individual working alone and separately from others. Although group work has become a more common feature of classroom organization in recent years, the stress on the individual has continued, so that achievement is measured in the nature of the individual's contribution rather than in the process of cooperation or the collective end result.

Many of us find working with others more difficult than working on our own. Because we have been trained to place reliance on our individuality, to watch our backs and to be wary of the intentions of others, we tend to see group work as yet another arena for competition. Cooperating with others on a common task requires additional skills, qualities and attitudes than those we bring to individual work. The approaches outlined in the following chapters can also be used effectively with pupils, giving them early experience of collaborative management.

In addition to the creation of conditions conducive to participation and cooperation, it is necessary to look for opportunities when collaborative working in groups is likely to produce more satisfying learning experiences and more productive learning outcomes.

Accountability

It is clear that the hard-edged accountability introduced through recent legislation will not produce the improvements expected of it. It is curious that the government so often promotes self-regulation, but favours a punitive inspection system for schools. Accountability involves the creation of a relationship of trust between individuals and groups of people, where the nature of the trust is explicitly stated and agreed. In the classroom it is desirable to develop a climate of mutual accountability between teacher and pupils, helping to establish an appropriate structure for learning and teaching. This process involves:

- negotiating agreements;
- making explicit statements of learning aims and purposes;
- working within agreed structures and boundaries;
- working to timetables and meeting deadlines;
- providing appropriate accounts of work done and results achieved.

This style of mutual accountability involves a dynamic interplay between teacher and learner:

- *The teacher* defines requirements, resources, time available and support.
- *The learner* expresses specific needs, particular interests and individual hopes.
- *Together they* agree the terms of reference for a piece of work, a programme of study, a curriculum assignment or a learning task.

Learners are more able to exercise accountability effectively when the teacher has helped them to:

- define precise learning purposes for each piece of work undertaken;
- create a clear vision of what the tangible end results of the piece of work will look like and the specifications that have been agreed;
- determine the discrete activities that will be needed to complete the work;
- produce a plan of the sequence of these activities;
- review the outcomes when the work is completed.

What often happens on the completion of a piece of work is that the teacher assesses and makes judgements about the work. This can discourage accountability, inhibit self-responsibility and reinforce dependence on the teacher. Learners are more likely to develop self-discipline, reliance and a real sense of responsibility if the teacher engages with them in a mutual examination of completed work, where the precise agreements between the teacher and the learner become an essential part of the evaluative process.

Pupil-profiling and records of achievement are important ingredients in this process of mutual accountability, although they are very much the summative part of it. Effective accountability is built, exercised and developed through the daily interactions of classroom life.

Primary schools have demonstrated their considerable capacity to take issues of organizational culture seriously. Although external pressure will continue to focus on the more hard-edged aspects of school life, we have to make sure that we give constant attention to building and developing human environments within which success and achievement become more likely.

◆6◆ GETTING THINGS DONE

As well as an effective management culture which creates the conditions in which people are helped to work creatively, schools also need to devise ways of translating organizational purposes into action to produce results. This is the realm of management strategy. In the years since the 1988 Education Reform Act, a somewhat narrow strategy has been emphasized (see Fig. 6.1). In addition to this, the framework for the Inspection of Schools has highlighted specific aspects of strategy for the inspection purpose:

- standards of achievement;
- quality of education provided;
- efficiency with which resources are managed;
- spiritual, moral, social and cultural development of pupils.

When the educational process is defined in this instrumental and somewhat lifeless terminology, there is a danger that we lose touch with the very essence of schools – life, learning and growth. There is so little in all these requirements to inspire teachers who are committed to their work and ambitious for their pupils. Nor is there anything to lift the soul and focus on the awesome potential of the learners themselves. Halting the slide of primary education into pedestrianism and officialdom is a major challenge. It will require courage, ambition and imagination to devise strategies for primary school development which are both quality-focused and life-enhancing.

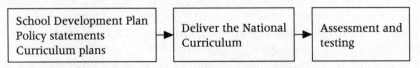

Figure 6.1 Managing a primary school: Narrow strategy.

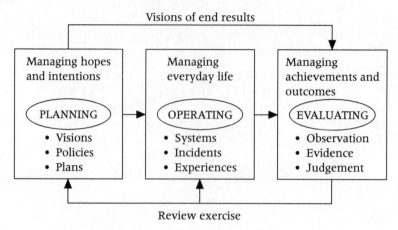

Figure 6.2 Managing a primary school: Broad strategy.

Given the complexities of modern life, it is necessary to devise an overall strategic model to guide the work of the school, and to help staff to work together in a systematic and cohesive way. The following strategic framework in Fig. 6.2 is offered as an example. This model conceives of a dynamic process of management in which all levels of school life can be reflected. The model can be used in a variety of ways:

- as a model for whole-school planning;
- as a framework for whole-school review;
- as a guide to the strategic work of governors and staff;
- to define roles and responsibilities;
- to build programmes of professional development;
- as a conceptual model of classroom life;
- as a basis for curriculum planning;
- as a guide to classroom organization;
- as a personal planning framework;
- by pupils to guide their self-directed learning.

Let us consider the various locations on this strategic map.

MANAGING HOPES AND INTENTIONS

In schools in recent years, there has been an increasing emphasis on planning, and there is now a confusing plethora of terms and phrases which refer to the management of intentions: dreams, visions, mission statements, the big idea, global policy, strategic purpose, values statement, action plans, programmes, plans, targets, goals, aims and objectives. While there are no standard definitions to provide security, it is important to

Table 6.1 Managing hopes and intentions

Layer 1	Layer 2	Layer 3
Vision	Dreams	Glimpses of the future in which our professional yearnings and aspirations find fulfilment
	Visions	Deliberately created mental pictures of the future, expressed in terms of 'how we want it to be'
Policy	Mission	Deliberately stated intentions to work towards specific aspects of the vision
	Policies	Statements of commitment and belief to a particular course of action
Plans	Programme	Detailed outlines of the development tasks to be accomplished in a given time
	Plan	Specifications listing intentions and action steps to accomplish the programme and serve the policy
	Aims, objectives, goals, targets	Largely interchangeable terms for specific and concrete intentions within a particular plan

place them within some framework of meaning if planning work is to be systematic and purposeful.

There are many means through which we can view the future and our intentions for it. The framework in Table 6.1 outlines a three-layer emphasis. Recent strictures have emphasized the specific and more action-focused aspect of the development process, yet any plan which is devoid of the professional passions contained in dreams and visions is unlikely to satisfy the hopes raised for it.

While the word 'vision' describes a school's idea of how it wants things to be, the term is also used to provide a powerful and motivating sense of direction. Peter Senge (1990: 217–18) observes:

> Visions that are truly shared take time to emerge. They grow as a by-product of interactions of individual visions. Experience suggests that visions that are genuinely shared require ongoing conversation where individuals not only feel free to express their dreams, but learn how to listen to each other's dreams. Out of this listening, new insights into what is possible gradually emerge.

This suggests that the current, somewhat pedestrian view of planning needs to be revitalized with the sorts of dreams and visions about schools that primary school educators are familiar. Edward Simon (quoted in Senge 1990: 348) notes:

Traditional organizations change by reacting to events. The reason for this, I think, is that the 'reference points' for traditional organizations are external, outside ourselves. Usually these reference points are the way things were in the past. Sometimes they include the way our competitors operate. Change means giving up these reference points. So, naturally, it is resisted. To be vision led means that our reference points are internal, the visions of the future we will create, not what we were in the past or what our competitors are doing. Only when it is vision led will an organization embrace change.

Although referring to business organizations, Simon warns us all of the dangers of sacrificing too much professional integrity to the external 'reference points'. The successful future of primary schools will depend on highly committed staff, working to strongly held visions about how things should be in the classrooms of a rapidly changing world.

The development of a vision-conscious staff, focusing on a powerful set of personal ambitions, and sharing in the big ideas of the organization as a whole, is a key challenge for headship. Such a vision-conscious staff is able to draw upon a set of deeply held ideas and convictions about the aims and purposes of the school, and a set of values about what matters, what is worth fighting for and what is not to be compromised. This does not mean that the external 'reference points' can be ignored, but rather that they need to be incorporated into a school's own visionary framework.

In their study of successful organizations, Tom Peters and Robert Waterman (1982) discovered a phenomenon in highly achieving companies which they defined as 'simultaneous loose/tight properties'. The tight bit is the determination to involve everyone in the building of the vision; the loose bit lies in the ability of each individual to make personal decisions about style and operation that will best enable that vision to be achieved. Many organizations operate this loose/tight phenomenon the other way round, with a looseness and vagueness about values and direction, but a rigidity in the way people are managed, and tightness around petty rules and regulations which managers enforce with a ruthless and relentless attention to duty.

It is perhaps only when personal visions and organizational visions comfortably combine that the optimum conditions for school success are created. There is much new work to be done here as the shift to a more optimistic and life-enhancing work ethic is built. One thing is certain, the continuation of traditional work assumptions in a world of increasing pressure and fast change is a recipe for disaster. In the end, the single factor that has to be faced is one of trust, and how we can build it in a world which has placed so much store in suspicion. The future depends upon management work of the highest quality, where courageous leaders work with patience and passion to build the visions from which high-quality schools will flow.

Building organizational vision

Perhaps the most significant challenge presented by the process of building a shared vision lies in the traditional assumptions about how organizational direction and decision-making are best managed. The view tends to be that it is leaders who have vision, and it is followers who need to fall into line behind it. In primary schools, the process of headteacher selection is very much about putting applicants' visionary perspectives under the microscope, and assessing the extent to which they have the necessary leadership skills and capacities to rally the staff behind them.

One of the key themes behind recent trends towards staff participation and involvement in planning and decision-making has been the belief that such involvement increases commitment among staff to organizational goals. This simplistic view is to misunderstand the motivation of people, and their capacity to give themselves to causes that are not always in their own best interests. Far too often compliance with management is mistaken for commitment, with damaging consequences.

A vision for the future of the school needs to resonate with the professional aspirations and beliefs of each member of staff. This cannot be achieved without the active participation of all staff as vision-builders. This does not mean that senior staff are helpless in the process. Clearly, they are accountable for the boundaries and principles which give the organization its existence, and for explaining contractual obligations and the nature of governance. It is also a necessary function of senior staff to set the agenda for vision-building, and to create the conditions within which all members of staff can willingly bring their own ideas about the future of the school.

Working simply to plans creates a management version of painting by numbers. We do end up with a picture but with prepackaged colours and somebody else's drawing. It lacks those most vital of ingredients: artistic integrity and individual creativity. On the other hand, relying simply on a vision can leave too much to chance and raises the temptation to revise the vision when action fails to realize it. It is sad that the recent preoccupation with planning has concentrated exclusively on the creation of targets that can be articulated without ambiguity. Nowhere have the big ideas of education been focused on – the fundamental purposes in human development and aspiration that learning serves.

Vision-building enables the staff of a primary school to create and develop an internalized disposition to serve the principles and values of the organization. The surest way to determine whether an organization has a vision is to walk into it and ask the people who work there what

Figure 6.3 Dimensions of school organization.

it is. If they refer you to the head's office or provide a series of inconsistent replies, then clearly there has not been a cohesive and concerted effort to build a set of agreed values and principles. But if you get a clear and consistently similar response about values and vision, you can be assured there is a sense of shared endeavour and a united effort towards agreed goals and targets.

MANAGING EVERYDAY LIFE

It is only necessary to spend a short time in a primary school to appreciate the complexity of the organizational process. Despite a constant stream of unexpected incidents and events, primary schools run smoothly, maintain the safety of their young children and go about their business with an air of purposeful calm. A whole range of systems and procedures underpin the management of daily life. Even a cursory analysis produces ten significant dimensions (see Fig. 6.3), each of which consists of an intricate network of issues, concerns, systems, procedures, tasks, regulations and processes. Not only does the organization of them require imagination and proficiency, it needs constant and careful attention to detail. In recent years, each of these dimensions has been affected by two types of change:

1 *Regulatory change*: changes brought about by legislation, regulation and requirement.

2 *Developmental change*: changes to daily life brought about by developments in social trends and habits, technological advances, environmental change and market forces.

Even before issues of learning and teaching can be addressed, it is necessary to establish a basic organizational framework with which all members of the organization are familiar. Good primary schools are models of efficiency, demonstrating considerable skill and imagination in managing this complex infrastructure.

As these organizational dimensions become more complex and demanding, it will be necessary to consider how they can best be managed within the staffing resources available. Current pressures and demands already force a distinction between educational management (i.e. the strategic work involved in planning, organizing and evaluating the learning life of the school) and organizational management (i.e. the work required to manage the dimensions outlined above). Headteachers have always accepted the duality of their responsibilities, but so complex and demanding have they now become, that there is a danger that educational leadership will need to be sacrificed. Many primary school heads experience enormous frustration and considerable stress as they struggle to reconcile these two vital, but distinct aspects of school life. Possible solutions to this growing problem lie in three directions.

Functional staffing

This involves moving away from the current distinction between teaching and non-teaching staff (imagine being a 'non' anything) and building a school staff according to the functions that need to be carried out. This will involve the introduction into school management of specialists in such areas as financial management, administration, premises management and pupil welfare. Large schools are already moving in this direction, recognizing that one way to enable those with purely educational responsibilities to concentrate entirely on their core function, is to employ specialists in the organizational dimensions. Caretakers, clerks, ancillary assistants and school meals staff already undertake this work, but often on a part-time basis, with low status and with little involvement in the overall management of the school. Problems with funding may inhibit the easy development of this particular solution, but the future is likely to see a less elitist distinction between teaching staff and others.

Organic management

Organic management requires all teaching members of staff to have responsibility portfolios reflecting three distinct aspects of school management: teaching, educational leadership and organizational management (this is considered more fully in Chapter 7). In practice, all teaching members of staff would become active co-managers in the whole organization, spreading the load throughout the staff team, rather than separating it out, with the majority of organizational responsibilities falling on the head and deputy head. This would enable senior members of staff to bring their experience and expertise more significantly into the educational domain, without the enormous pressures that result from performing a plethora of organizational functions.

This does not mean extra work for teachers, rather a reconfiguring of all the work that has to be carried out to enable the school to function effectively. It offers a management strategy built on small, often temporary teams, moving into action as and when specific organizational tasks are required. Such an approach would mean that, in addition to class teaching responsibilities and work on educational development projects, each member of staff would work from time to time in the organizational domain, working in a team with one or two others to tackle both routine and developmental tasks.

Federal management

This solution may be particularly important for smaller primary schools. Rather than attempt to undertake all their management work separately from all other schools, groups would be formed to provide mutual support and development opportunities. When a curriculum innovation needs to be planned, for example, a project team consisting of three or four teachers from certain schools in the federal structure would work together on behalf of all the schools in the group. Combined INSET days could be used for wider consultation, professional development, planning and evaluation.

If each school agreed to contribute a per capita proportion of its staffing budget to a federal account, the employment of part- or full-time specialists would be possible, creating a federal staffing structure with both flexibility and appropriate specialism within it. Many of the contracts could be for a fixed term, for example for the life of a particular project. Employment arrangements in the future, with a higher proportion of people in self-employment, semi-retirement and consultancy-style jobs, will make this approach particularly attractive.

It is through daily activity that the school culture is developed. The sorts of syntropic cultures outlined in Chapter 5 are not created simply by policies, plans and operating systems. They are developed through the interweaving of the values we demonstrate in our work, and the ways we manage our interpersonal relationships with pupils and colleagues as we respond to the various incidents and events of the school day. Much will depend upon how individuals deal with crises, respond to difficulty and pressure, and how they handle success and achievement.

MANAGING ACHIEVEMENTS AND OUTCOMES

The recent focus on the evaluation of schools has helped to highlight the importance of using carefully designed processes and procedures to check whether plans made for children's learning compare favourably with outcomes. This focus, however, has a number of serious problems. First, it has established a view that teachers and schools have not been concerned with evaluation, and that they do not know how to do it. This is deeply insulting to a profession which probably does more on-the-job evaluation than almost any other. Teaching is impossible without knowing how individual learners are progressing, or being aware of the outcomes of different teaching methods and techniques. Secondly, the mechanistic approach to evaluation which has been adopted, places disproportionate emphasis on hard-edged, statistically measurable data. This is to assume that the more elusive aspects of pupil learning are not important because they are not as easily evaluated. Thirdly, evaluation has been presented as an event-driven activity rather than a continual process. This is to diminish the importance of implicit evaluation in the management of learning. In the years ahead, we will need to abandon this obsession with the mechanistic and instrumental, and devise more useful systems of evaluation which will provide us with a whole range of insights and information, rather than a simple and narrow set of scores.

The broad approach to strategy outlined in Fig. 6.2 places evaluation in a dynamic process. The review exercise indicated by the backward flowing arrows suggests a systematic comparison of outcomes and intentions. The strategy can be applied to large-scale exercises like the school development plan, as well as to smaller-scale activities within specific curriculum areas or pupils' own learning programmes. It involves using the documented descriptions of the end results specified for a particular development, and relating these to the outcomes that have been produced. This will establish one of three possible positions:

1 Outcomes are commensurate with intentions.
2 Outcomes exceed intentions.
3 Outcomes fall short of intentions.

If outcomes are largely as planned, this indicates successful planning and implementation. The school will want to consider whether some raising of aims and expectations will bring even greater success, or whether the costs of producing such outcomes have been disproportionate to the resources available and cannot be sustained in the future. If the outcomes have exceeded the intentions, then it will be important to establish why this was the case. Perhaps the intentions were too modest, in which case the planning may need to be reviewed. Perhaps the methodologies used were more effective than expected, in which case these will need to be examined to identify the precise causes of success so that these can be more widely adopted. Similarly, if outcomes are short of intentions, then it will be necessary to consider whether planning was too ambitious, or if problems arose in the implementation and operational stage.

In defining the processes involved in evaluation, we need to bear in mind the difference in operational practice between two distinct approaches:

1 *Event evaluation*: conducting evaluation as a set of precise, scheduled exercises, often managed with objectivity in mind.
2 *Process evaluation*: using evaluation as part of an integrative strategic process which is taking place all the time. It values both subjective and objective data in the constant search for insight and understanding.

It is this second approach which we need build into our management processes. Figure 6.2 suggests three particular aspects of the process: observation, evidence and judgement.

Observation

Observation is often regarded as a deliberate and discrete activity that takes place intermittently in schools. It evokes images of clip boards, observation schedules and trying to be separate from what is being observed. This sort of observation can be a very useful exercise when particular information is required, but it is by no means the only approach. It is through the implicit process of observing what is happening as we conduct the day-to-day business of the organization, that we gain the vast majority of information about how things are going. We do not require trained observers to tell us whether it is a 'wet playtime' or whether a child is on-task. We know these things through our constant awareness of what is happening. It is too easy to dismiss this awareness as entirely subjective, but then most of what happens in learning is. We need to appreciate that it is through our conscious awareness that we acquire the information we need to manage our affairs.

This implicit type of observation can be described as 'skilled noticing'. It involves using our observational skills as we go about our classroom work in a directed and precise way, searching for information that can tell us about progress and development. We need to develop the habit of capturing and recording significant incidents and behaviour, information that can be used later to help us form judgements about achievements and outcomes. If we have done our planning work well, we will have specified, often in some detail, the exact nature of the outcomes we are working towards, and we will be alert to signs that they are being achieved.

Evidence

We need evidence to judge effectiveness. Just as in courts of law, this evidence needs to be specific, detailed and factual. Impressions and opinions are not sufficient grounds to assure us that the conclusions we draw about the quality of our work are safe and secure. The systematic gathering of evidence involves four particular sources:

- *Observation*: what we see and hear.
- *Enquiry*: evidence gained through dialogue with learners and others.
- *Material*: pupils' work, documents and records.
- *Measurements*: the results of assessments, sampling and testing.

Judgement

It is not until appropriate data are assembled that evaluation can take place. This part of the process requires judgements to be made in relation to the intentions originally specified. The key question is: Have we done what we set out to do? We can only answer this when we have made a rigorous comparison between the specified aims and the manifest outcomes. The accuracy of the judgements will not only depend upon the range and quality of the evidence assembled, but also on the thoroughness of the observational work we engage in and record.

Well-managed evaluation is vital to enable us to identify our strengths and difficulties, to know where to plan new initiatives, where to provide more support and where to spread the techniques of effective practice.

Self-managed evaluation

The future will demand that we become more evaluation-conscious than we have tended to be in the past. We need to become more systematic about our management of the whole of the strategic process and to invest more time and energy to the planning and evaluation parts of the strategy, currently in very short supply in our primary schools. If the government was really imaginative about improving educational standards, it would realize the need to provide schools with significantly more preparation and review time than is currently available. Reorganizing the attendance times of pupils to allow this would help to improve the quality of management and learning considerably.

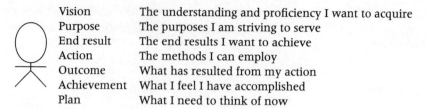

Vision	The understanding and proficiency I want to acquire
Purpose	The purposes I am striving to serve
End result	The end results I want to achieve
Action	The methods I can employ
Outcome	What has resulted from my action
Achievement	What I feel I have accomplished
Plan	What I need to think of now

Figure 6.4   Framework for self-managed learning.

We also need to give a new emphasis to self-managed evaluation. Pupils, like their teachers, are skilled noticers of what goes on around them and they are very capable of making perceptive judgements about their own learning. Although they are inevitably involved in self-assessment, this is not regarded as appropriate, relevant or important. It is sad that the OFSTED framework provides no significant place for the gathering of data from pupils themselves.

It is the learners themselves who have the greatest interest in learning. We need to help them to build skills in assessment and evaluation in order that they can operate the strategic approach for themselves. Developing pupil skills in evaluation will facilitate the journey from dependence to interdependence, encouraging a more formative sense of self-responsibility than is presently encouraged in the schooling system. Self-evaluation is a vital component in the process of becoming, of systematically unfolding our potentialities in the world.

Pupils from the very earliest years in primary schools can be helped to acquire and build their self-evaluation skills. A simple framework like that outlined in Fig. 6.4 would provide a useful basis. Helping pupils to take a more active and responsible role in the evaluation of their learning will help them to develop other skills and qualities. By becoming more self-aware and curious about the nature of their own learning, they will develop greater clarity in defining their own learning purposes, thus making their approach to learning more purposeful. They will also apply more thought and attention to getting themselves organized for learning. In reflecting on the nature of their learning experiences, they will have a more substantial framework to guide them, and will undoubtedly increase their capacity to make accurate and illuminating evaluations of their own achievements.

School evaluation

An evaluation-conscious school will always be anxious for feedback about how it is doing. All members of the school – staff and pupils alike – will be alert to evidence that things are going according to plan. Evaluation is a process of exploration, a way of discovering the sometimes hidden meanings behind what happens. In good schools, it is driven by a powerful curiosity about the intricacies of learning and teaching and by a relentless need for insight and understanding. It must never become only an event, conducted when things appear to be going wrong. Good evaluation is the key to doing the right things.

MANAGING DEVELOPMENT PROJECTS

On their own, visions do not change the world or make a primary school more effective. Big ideas need to be translated into practical action if that is to be achieved. It is the transforming of ideas into effects that is challenging, and perhaps the most significant characteristic of effective primary schools is their capacity to implement successful changes and to achieve consistently high-quality outcomes.

Most of us are good at changing things when there is a need and we stand to benefit, but organizational change requires more than individual and idiosyncratic approaches to improvement, it needs concerted and collective cohesion and a well-practised strategy.

One of the challenges of development work in schools lies in the tradition of teachers working in classrooms, separated from their colleagues. This often means that when it is necessary to work in more collective arrangements, autonomy and the individualistic tendency do not make collaboration easy and straightforward. Good teamwork demands a great deal of give-and-take and some sacrificing of personal predilections if it is to succeed. In the years ahead, as we struggle with the evolutionary crisis, organizational effectiveness will increasingly rely on our skills and capacities in collaborative management. Success at this will depend on the staff as a whole being prepared to see training and development in teamwork as a central pillar of their professional development programme.

In the confusion and uncertainty that is created by fast and accelerating change, it is important to develop systems and structures that will help us to navigate successfully through the challenges and complexities of primary school development. Murgatroyd (1988) has described four different ways an organization can respond to changing needs and circumstances:

1 *Chaotic*: in which the organization responds to change in an unstructured and fruitless way.
2 *Standard*: in which the organization responds with a routine procedure and is reluctant to use new or risky strategies.
3 *Rigid*: in which the organization responds in a fixed way – usually *No!*
4 *Flexible*: in which the organization responds in a considered way with imagination and flexibility as events unfold.

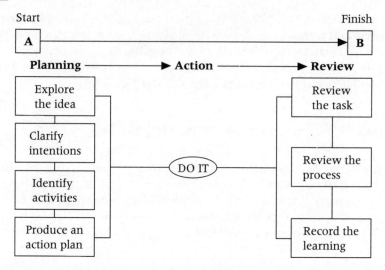

Figure 6.5 Framework for project management.

Clearly, the last of these is preferable and in order to achieve the considered and imaginative approach described, it is necessary to devise ways of achieving the flexibility and imagination required.

Development projects need to be managed through a systematic process which all members of staff are familiar with and experienced in. Turbulent times require that we do not waste time inventing procedures every time a new project comes along. The model in Fig. 6.5 is offered as an example. It has been used successfully on a wide range of projects and tasks. It is seldom a good idea to simply adopt what works for other people. It is much better to note the principles and then experiment, to devise a model that grows out of the skills and experience of the particular staff team. The key principles of this framework are planning, action and review.

Planning

Since it is the action stage which enables the journey from A (where we are now) to B (where we want to be) to be undertaken, it is vital that the action serves the purposes of the project and brings about the outcomes desired. Action time can be reduced considerably if the planning is done well. One of the secrets of the successful management of teamwork is to resist the temptation of entering the action phase too quickly – drafting reports, making decisions, designing teaching programmes or planning arrangements, for example. Attention to detail in planning means that when eventually the action stage is reached, the work can be tackled with confidence, with a minimum of fuss and without the uncertainties and anxieties that often attend badly planned ventures.

Exploring the idea

Essentially, this is an initial period of contemplation and consultation which allows all those involved to get to know about the proposed project and to consider its implication, both for the school as a whole and for each member of staff.

Many projects flounder because insufficient thought and imagination is given to the announcement of the idea, informing everyone who needs to know and providing sufficient information for people to consider the implications. Time needs to be provided for questions to be asked, points of view expressed, potential difficulties explored and possible costs and benefits to be assessed. Dialogue needs to be encouraged so that everyone can become involved, express their opinions, share their ideas and influence events. Once these initial explorations have been carried out, more specific preparations are required.

Clarifying intentions

It is vital to define a development project as a task. Far too often changes are articulated in passive and general language: 'We need to improve staff communication'. Such a project statement is vague and open-ended. It can generate feelings of confusion, uncertainty and anxiety with such responses as, 'What does that mean?'. The key lies in the presence and choice of verbs: 'To improve' conveys a general hope that something can be done and 'communication' is an all encompassing term for a whole range of activities.

What is required is a statement that provides a clear indication of what is intended: 'Devise at least three practical strategies to ensure that all members of staff are briefed about weekly events'. This second definition has closed the task down to a very specific aspect of communication, and has indicated what has to be done – the devising of practical strategies. When tasks are defined like this, they tend to create more clarity and understanding, and produce relevant suggestions and practical ideas. They also focus on action, on getting something done.

The process of project clarification can be helped in two ways in particular. First, it is important to ensure that everyone involved understands the purposes of the project. If you ask the question, 'Why are you doing this project?', you will probably receive the answer, 'Because communications are bad'. This refers to the past and does not help to create a sense of purpose. If you ask people to complete the sentence, 'We are doing this project in order to . . .', then you tend to get purposes about a preferable future. One of the surest ways to create problems in the later stages of a project's life is to avoid or rush the process of purpose clarification. When everyone begins with the same idea in mind, then cohesion and effective progress are more likely.

The second way to facilitate clarity of intention is to specify the intended outcomes of the project. This is the vision part of project planning and involves the listing of all significant responses to the sentence which begins, 'What we will end up with is . . .'.

Producing useful responses involves projecting the mind forward into the future to visualize what intended outcomes will look like. The greater the detail that can be supplied to this envisioning, the clearer the path towards achieving them will be. A project vision statement describes the ways we want things to be when we have successfully completed the task. The statement will contain images of how things will look, how they are organized, what people are doing, what systems are in operation, what skills and qualities are being used, specific roles, materials and resources, cultural factors and the outcomes and effects that have been achieved.

Statements of purpose and end result should be written down and circulated to all project participants' as they are vital documents which record the intentions and aspirations for the project being undertaken.

Identifying activities

Managing a development project is a precarious business, requiring a capacity to understand the organizational dynamics at work. This involves the ability to identify potential entry points for action and to recognize blocks to development and growth. Too often development projects are hindered because vital information is ignored or not taken sufficiently seriously. While the earlier planning phases will bring most information into consideration, it is very important to analyse the forces that can be used to assist the forward movement of the project, and those which may emerge to inhibit it.

The diagnostic device shown in Fig. 6.6 was developed from Kurt Lewin's (1936) celebrated 'Force/Field' technique. It suggests that a development project is poised between two sets of opposing forces – the forces that may work *for* the development and the forces that may work *against* it. In preparing and planning the project, it is necessary to identify the dynamics of the relationship between helping and hindering forces. It is sometimes more profitable to look to the hindering forces first, and devise ways to work on them so as to create a more conducive climate for change and development. A capacity to sense these dynamics and to identify accurately appropriate stances and entry points is essential if we are to navigate through the powerful dynamics that operate in

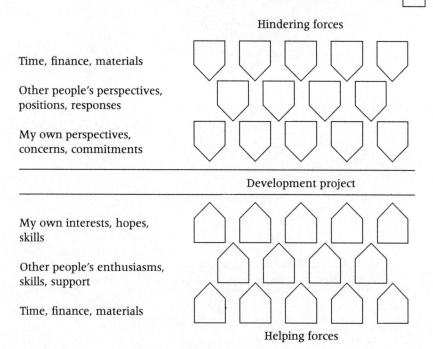

Hindering forces

Time, finance, materials

Other people's perspectives,
positions, responses

My own perspectives,
concerns, commitments

Development project

My own interests, hopes,
skills

Other people's enthusiasms,
skills, support

Time, finance, materials

Helping forces

Figure 6.6   Project analysis.

most organizations. Simply activating the helping forces can sometimes create too strong a wave of change and can cause resentment and threaten the project itself. Such an analysis can be undertaken by individuals using printed forms similar to that shown in Fig. 6.6, or carried out in groups round a flip chart or white board. This will generate lively discussion, further enabling the complexities of the various forces to be teased out and understood.

What the project analysis will do is to identify a range of discrete activities that will have to be undertaken. If, for example, the active support of the headteacher has been specified as one of the helping forces, then it will be necessary to activate this support and give it shape and direction. Enlisting the head's support thus becomes a target, and engaging in dialogue to secure that support will be the activity that is required to achieve it.

It is only when we have clarified the forces at work in relation to the project that we are in a position to set specific targets and specify the activities necessary to achieve them. The distinction between targets and activities is illustrated in Fig. 6.7. What will be required before final planning can take place is a list of all the activities that will be necessary in the action phase of the project. The planning matrix shown in Fig. 6.8 will help to assemble all the factors which need to be considered:

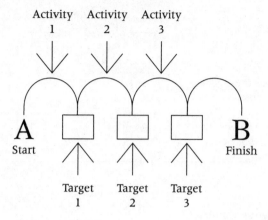

Figure 6.7 Targets and activities.

Target	Activity	How	Who	When	End result

Figure 6.8 Project planning matrix.

1 Specify the targets which will need to be achieved.
2 List the activities which will need to be undertaken.
3 Note the methods to be used.
4 Identify people involved and their specific roles.
5 Indicate when the activity will be scheduled and the deadline.
6 Specify the nature of the end result.

  Like the earlier project analysis, this task can be undertaken by individuals using printed sheets to record their ideas or in a group session using a flip chart or white board. Group planning is useful to produce the overall activity list and identify key people who will lead particular activities. Individual sheets can then be used by those who have particular responsibilities.

Producing an action plan

The final stage before action is to synthesize all previous phases into an action plan for the project. This will involve decisions about which order the activities need to be conducted in, and whether these are sequential or can be managed concurrently. While individuals will want to create their own planning documents, it is useful to have a master plan showing the critical path through the various activities. Having such a plan on the wall can provide a focus for reviews, team briefings and for recording progress to date. While a range of computer software is available to help the process of project management, simple diagrams tend to work best, providing they convey clearly the essential elements of the action stage and the time-scale involved.

One of the challenges of effective planning is resisting the temptation to rush into action before sufficient preparation has been carried out. Working in an atmosphere of continual change means that we will have to improve our planning techniques if we are to get developments in place before further change makes their introduction unnecessary. Adopting a systematic approach and having a project manager who takes responsibility for the phases and stages of the development is absolutely vital if the work of individuals is to be well coordinated, and confidence in the management methodology acquired.

Action

When the planning is complete, those involved should be able to move smoothly and confidently from preparation into action. Action should never begin until everyone has a clear understanding of the overall plan and a very detailed appreciation of their own contribution, with targets and activities clearly set within an agreed time-scale.

Review

Although review usually follows the action stage, it is as important to the whole process as the other stages, but it is the one that tends to be avoided or neglected unless there is good leadership and review activities have been agreed in the action plan. It is through systematic and skilful reviewing that we can evaluate the effectiveness of our development projects while at the same time significantly increasing individual and organizational awareness about the management process, the successful contributions of individuals, the management of difficulties and unexpected hindrances, and the usefulness of the action plan itself.

While a major review will be essential on completion of a development project, interim reviews will be useful throughout the process and form an excellent way of taking stock, assessing progress, noting unexpected incidents and events, adjusting time-scales, reallocating resources and redefining priorities. No project in the complex world of primary school management can ever go perfectly to plan, and brief interim

What we did that was successful	What we can do to repeat this success in the future
What we did that created difficulties	What we can do to overcome these difficulties in the future
Specific contributions that were especially helpful	Individual skills we need to develop

Figure 6.9 A process review.

reviews conducted regularly throughout the project's progress will help to keep everyone focused and well informed. Two types of review are suggested: task review and process review.

Task review

Task reviews enable us to compare outcomes with intentions and to measure the effectiveness of a project in terms of its achievements. One of the very great benefits of the end result statements generated in the intention clarifying stage of the planning process, is that clear specifications of outcomes have been made and can be used as checking devices. The purpose of interim task reviews is to prevent difficulties becoming compounded, and to allow for adjustments and fine-tuning to the action plan.

Process review

Process reviews are concerned with the conduct and management of the project, and focus on how the different stages of the project cycle were managed, how leadership was achieved, how team relationships worked and how particular methods and techniques were used. A useful way to review the process is to produce forms designed to encourage reflective thinking about the process (see Fig. 6.9).

Time for review should be allocated on the completion of a task, or at any time the team wants to give attention to its process. After a few minutes of reflection to make notes on the forms, it is useful to hold a discussion about each of the categories on the form. Take each point in turn and then allow a few minutes discussion on matters arising. In terms of process, the aims of the process review are to:

1 Share feelings about the task and its management.
2 Highlight successes and difficulties.
3 Identify areas for team development.
4 Provide feedback to individual team members.
5 Make plans for future teamwork.
6 Appreciate the process of working together.
7 Identify areas for individual development.
8 Build confidence and team spirit.
9 Develop the organizational culture.
10 Help the school work towards its vision.

Recording the learning

Every project we undertake is an opportunity to learn more about the complexities of primary school leadership and management. The most valuable resource of any organization is a management or project team that is constantly reviewing itself and incorporating practices which it has discovered or refined in the course of its work. Such a team is always interested in how to do things better next time, constantly fascinated by methodology and techniques and anxious to share the team's insights with other teams and individuals.

In managing the strategic development of a primary school, two issues are important if both effectiveness and efficiency are to be achieved. The first is to devise a systematic framework which can be used consistently to tackle management tasks. Using the framework in the many different ways suggested earlier, increases familiarity with its processes and procedures, ensuring that urgent tasks can be achieved promptly, and complex tasks approached thoroughly. This will involve all participants in learning the procedures and developing their skills through practice. The review element in the framework is the key to this, and those managing projects should ensure that regular review becomes the heart of the whole process.

The second issue is to do with the use of teams and task groups in the developmental work of the school, and this is the subject of Chapter 7.

◆7◆ TEAMWORK AND COLLABORATION

In the context of rapid and accelerating change, it is no longer sensible to run effective organizations which rely on separation and individualism. Survival and effectiveness depend upon those working in organizations to discover and develop more efficient and effective ways of satisfying the numerous, varied and continual work demands that are created. Much of the stress experienced in organizations comes from the fact that in too many situations, members of the same organization seem to be competing with each other rather than collaborating.

One of the inherited organizational principles of schooling is individualism, and the single teacher and the class of learners has become established as the fundamental work unit in schools. The curriculum is built around this notion, the timetable organizes it and work is allocated on the basis of it. This notion has also extended to the management of primary schools, so that individual teachers have been required to take leadership and coordination responsibilities for a subject area.

Ray Krok (1977) has coined the phrase 'None of us is as good as all of us' to emphasize the enormous potential lying untapped and underused in most organizations, potential that only can be released by bringing individuals together in powerful work alliances, often temporary ones, to tackle the unending flow of tasks, projects and demands that arise daily in most schools. Increasing levels of stress suggest that traditional management structures are experiencing considerable difficulty in meeting new demands and changed circumstances. Collaboration has the capability of enabling most organizations to increase both their efficiency and their effectiveness.

In recent years, increasing pressure has changed the metabolism of primary schools, creating a range of challenges which are complex, confusing and difficult to meet. Constant and relentless attacks on professional integrity and performance, accompanied by massive changes in the regulations affecting the management and conduct of schools, have driven teachers into a crisis of confidence and effectiveness, lowering morale and increasing stress.

The combination of pressures from increased prescriptions and heightened expectations has brought about some significant effects in schools:

- increase in the weight of individual workloads;
- increase in the complexity of workloads;
- too little time for too many changes;
- the confusion of managing many significant changes simultaneously;
- lack of time for preparation, adjustment and training;
- changes changed again before being implemented;
- increase in confusion, uncertainty, ambiguity and turbulence;
- panic to cover the ground with insufficient attention to detail;
- further erosion of professional time into personal time at the expense of individual well-being and family life.

Management structures built on individual and separated responsibility are placing disproportionate pressure on some teachers, who often feel overwhelmed by the demands placed on them and experience painful feelings of isolation, inadequacy and panic. If left unchecked and unattended to, these can lead to both personal and professional dysfunction.

Accompanying the myriad of changes in society have been significant developments in the theory and practice of management and leadership. The 1980s saw a steady growth in understanding about organizations and how they work. Central to this was a growing realization that members of organizations tend to work more effectively and efficiently when certain conditions are satisfied. Many companies began to move away from structures which tended to differentiate workers from each other and moved towards more fluid organizational arrangements designed for flexibility and change. There was a growing recognition that the experience accumulated by workers in organizations can be used productively to serve management needs, and that by increasing the management partnership, problems are easier to solve and change more comfortable to accomplish.

THE TEAMWORK OPTION

Building a teamwork approach to school management is not straightforward, and we will need to take it in small steps. Experimenting with teams of two is most likely to show the value of collaboration and introduce a new spirit of cooperation and collegiality. Staff will need to learn new collaborative skills as they carry out new challenges. Few individuals in a school will ever have all the skills they need for the next innovation, and these will need to be acquired quickly, demanding a fresh look at how we manage professional development and training in schools. The notion of the learning organization underlines the idea that no organization in conditions of fast change can ever be fully prepared for new challenges. What will single out the successful organizations from the weaker ones is their capacity to learn fast and adapt.

The inevitable move towards collaboration does not mean that all work must be carried out in teams, groups or partnerships. A proper individualism is vital to the successful management of work and the effective use of human resources. What it does mean is a greater capacity to think collectively and utilize the skills and qualities of people in more creative and effective ways. When we think about teams we have a tendency to focus on sport and team games such as football, hockey and cricket. Other sports also have an important element of teamwork: golfing pairs, tennis doubles, rowing trios (i.e. the coxed pair). There is also one of the quintessential examples of effective collaboration to inspire us: the athlete and the coach.

There is much we can learn from these examples about teamwork in schools. But before we can become successful in large organizational groupings, we need to experience the challenges and pleasures of working in small teams of two or three.

FROM INDIVIDUALISM TO COLLABORATION

It is important to make a distinction between individuality and individualism. The first refers to the fact that any organization consists of a group of unique individuals, all with different experiences, skills, values and motivations. The challenge of organizational life is to bring this disparate group together into a cohesive team, so that they are able to meet the challenges that, separately, they would be less successful in responding to. Individualism, on the other hand, works on the assumption that each person has rights beyond the needs of the organization. This can result in an entrenched separation of individuals from the organizational whole. It is the tension between individualism and wholeness which is such a challenge for senior managers.

Studies of the capacity of organizations to change and adapt successfully have stressed the importance of culture and climate. It is useful to be on the lookout for signs of distress. These can include:

• excessive conflict not conducive to change;
• excessive consensus not conducive to change;
• repeated or unexpected poor performance in part of the organization by an individual or group;
• low morale;

- lack of concern among participants for their own professional development;
- high staff turnover;
- failure of the organization to challenge and question its own decisions;
- failure to carry out agreed and assigned work;
- excessive paper communication and management by memo;
- high level of absenteeism.

An understanding of these issues prevents unsuitable strategies from being advocated and unrealistic goals from being pursued.

The move to collaboration is very challenging for a number of reasons:

1 It is unfamiliar.
2 It has not been part of professional training and preparation.
3 It is a recent phenomenon in most organizations and certainly schools.
4 There is a fear of exposing professional inadequacies.

It is useful to conceive of three levels of work:

1 *Individual work*: work that we undertake alone, separated from our colleagues, including class teaching, report writing, planning, preparation, dealing with pupils and parents.
2 *Teamwork*: work that we undertake with particular colleagues, including departmental management, curriculum teams, working parties, appraisal partnerships, committees.
3 *Corporate work*: work involving the whole organization, such as full staff meetings and gatherings. In well-managed collaborative organizations, full staff meetings are usually called to receive the reports of subgroups and teams, and for some sharing of information.

It is in the second of these that the main challenges to management in the future lie.

Organizations that succeed in using team development as a key part of their management structure are the ones best poised to:

- make leaps in innovation;
- improve quality;
- increase efficiency;
- enhance performance.

Some of the issues that need to be resolved in moving to team development include:

1 *Relationship of teams to the school decision-making process.* To harness the potential of a primary school, it is vital to bring as many participants as possible into the co-management process, and to give them an active share in creating vision and policy, designing strategy, making decisions and evaluating effectiveness. Commitment to organizational

aims and aspirations can only be achieved where there is a close connection of individuals to the determination of policies and plans.

2 *The nature of authority invested in teams.* Teams need to be given real power and authority to manage tasks and projects. They need to be able to work without constant referral to senior managers, and encouraged to determine their own priorities, decide working methods and make appropriate decisions.

3 *Ground rules for team management.* Within an overall plan for team management, individual teams need opportunity and scope to experiment, to learn and to develop effective working practices. This means access to training in team development. There is no single correct way to run an effective management team, and flexibility, creativity and imagination need to be high priorities. It is important not to invest too high an expectation in team management too soon. Teams need to build confidence and develop skill through achievement and success. In the early stages of team management, tasks need to be clear, of short duration and within the capacity of the team to deliver.

TASK-FOCUSED MANAGEMENT

One of the significant shifts in working practice has been from fixed responsibility roles to flexible and responsive roles. In a climate of uncertainty, with new and unexpected tasks arising increasingly regularly, it makes no sense to tie people to fixed and rigid roles. Management structures need a new quality of *ad-hocracy*, the capacity to respond to new tasks quickly and efficiently. Fixed-role management can create severe difficulties for modern organizations:

1 It can create an imbalance in work. Some individuals can find themselves hugely overloaded, while others remain temporarily free of any major tasks.

2 Time allocations for changes are shorter than they were. Innovations have to be put in place much quicker.

3 Many of the tasks are such that previous experience is not guaranteed to help. There is a novelty to many innovations for which no ready expertise may exist.

Management activity needs to be less concerned with defining areas of responsibility and more concerned with what needs doing next. Senior managers in primary schools have found themselves disproportionately challenged by change because of the novelty of new tasks and challenges. Staff already have full and extensive portfolios of responsibility so that senior staff have no choice but to take on more themselves. What is required is a new concept, a new way of managing.

In most primary schools today, in virtually all responsibility areas, there is more work than individuals can ever hope to accomplish. There are two ways forward:

1 We will have to be tougher about priorities. This will involve deciding not to do some things at all and deciding to carry out others to a more moderate level of achievement. The key decision will be about which tasks the school will really want to do well. A new ruthlessness about priorities will require courage and sensitive leadership. The new proverb, 'If a job is not worth doing well, it is not worth doing at all', will become increasingly significant.
2 We will need to develop new ways of allocating tasks and spreading the management workload. This will involve abandoning management practices that have served well in the past and learning to develop new management processes that will serve a change and changing future.

What this will mean in the short term, as we struggle to cope with increasing change, is that teachers will need to abandon some of their adherence to a special and separate area of responsibility and be ready, when needs demand, to dip in and out of small and temporary task teams. School management structures will need to be built on the notion of an annual round of significant management tasks. Bringing staff together to tackle these jobs and tasks will be the hallmark of flexible and adaptive management.

The types of team required will include:

- task interpretation teams,
- design teams,
- planning teams,
- start-up teams,
- action teams,
- development teams,
- completer teams,
- review teams,
- forecasting teams.

Senior staff need to recognize that to be effective, the school needs to involve all staff in both strategic and tactical management. This creates a more dynamic management culture, ensuring that all skills and qualities, not only those residing in senior staff, are incorporated into the collaborative endeavour. Future success will very much depend on the capabilities of teams to be innovative and they will require as much autonomy as possible. This team-based, collaborative structure becomes more like a network of relationships than a bureaucratic hierarchy. Co-ordination tends to be informal, allowing teams to experiment with process and procedure in pursuit of high-quality end results. Much energy

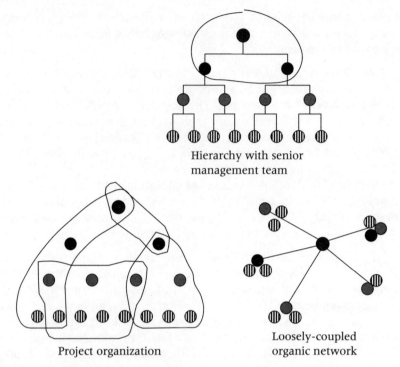

Hierarchy with senior
management team

Project organization

Loosely-coupled
organic network

Figure 7.1 Organizational forms.

is directed towards creating a shared understanding and appreciation of school developments, within and across project teams.

ORGANIZATIONAL FORMS

Gareth Morgan (1989) has charted the development of organizational structures, from traditional bureaucracies to what he describes as loosely coupled organic networks. Figure 7.1 provides three examples. Most primary schools have long since departed from the rigidly bureaucratic model, and many have moved towards some team structure, particularly through the identification of a senior management team. The ideas set out in this and the previous chapter suggest a model similar to that described by Morgan as a 'project organization'. The hierarchy still exists, but has remodelled itself as a number of project teams, drawing all members of staff into the management of school development. Some members, particularly senior ones, are members of more than one team.

The loosely coupled 'organic network' goes further, placing the head at the centre of a constantly changing pattern of small, task-focused temporary teams. The pattern changes according to the organizational and developmental needs of the moment. This more flexible, organic arrangement becomes possible when staff have become familiar with, and skilful in, management by project teams. The key feature is *ad hocracy* – teams are created, contingent on the current tasks and demands experienced within the school. A job of work becomes necessary, the task is defined, a team is set up, the job is done, the team disperses. Team membership is fluid and changes according to the task and availability of staff. Teams are more in the nature of temporary partnerships than ongoing committees. Teams can be set up quickly, and get their work done in shorter time spans than normal. Staff develop enormous flexibility and constantly widen their experience through regular opportunities to work with specialist colleagues and take on important leadership roles.

The idea that there is one ideal management structure is an outdated concept. The future will demand flexibility, and both effectiveness and efficiency will increasingly demand high skills in teamwork and collaboration. Yet it is by no means an easy process to change a bureaucratic management structure into an organic network. The changes required are more than structural, they are cultural and political as well. Much will depend on the skills and patience of senior staff to introduce developments that staff will welcome, and can be successful at. This will require a rebalancing of authority and power, and the relinquishing of senior control over decision-making and supervision. Development needs to build on incremental success.

BEING A TEAM MEMBER

Teams are made up of individuals, each with their own hopes and aspirations, as well as their worries and concerns. Three particular issues are important for most of us when we join a team:

- *Inclusion*: Will I feel involved and accepted?
- *Control*: How much influence will I have over what happens?
- *Affection*: Will the other team members like me?

The following list of questions will help to focus on these issues, and to raise awareness of the challenges and difficulties that can arise when people who do not have a great deal of experience in teams and groups are required to work in collaborative ways.

Inclusion
- What am I hoping for in this team?
- How do I want other team members to behave towards me?
- Do other team members include me in the process?

- Do they call me by name and invite my participation?
- Do they respond when I make suggestions?
- Do they tend to welcome my contributions?
- How am I feeling about my participation in this team?
- What have been the things I have enjoyed?
- What incidents have upset or worried me?

Control
- Who exerts the most influence in the team?
- How do I react to attempts to influence or control my behaviour in the team?
- Do I get *volunteered* for tasks? How do I react to this?
- How do others respond when I try and exert some influence in the team?
- Which people are more inclined to support my ideas and suggestions?
- Do some team members tend to oppose or try to block my influence?
- How do I behave when I feel the team is moving in directions I am not comfortable with? How do I register my concerns? How do others react when I do this?

Affection
- Do others in the team like me? What have individuals said or done that show that they do?
- How do each of the team members show their feelings towards me?
- How do I feel about my colleagues in the team?
- How do I express my feelings for those I like?
- How does the team handle disagreements and interpersonal conflicts?
- How do I express myself to particular individuals when what they say upsets me?

These issues are crucially important to the effectiveness and well-being of individuals in groups, yet they are rarely acknowledged as part of the necessary 'process' development of a team. We all bring important needs to teamwork, just as we do in other aspects of our work, and good teams develop a sensitive awareness of personal difficulties, worries and concerns. If team members are struggling to handle their feelings of being excluded, being controlled or being disliked, then the whole team is likely to suffer and the quality of the teamwork will be inhibited.

In developing the capabilities necessary to become an effective team member, it is useful to consider three types of responsibility: responsibility to self, team and school.

Responsibility to self

We each bring to our work in teams, groups and committees a range of resources: our experience, our skills and qualities, our knowledge and understanding and our sensitivity and awareness of others. We have the capacity to influence the team, to affect its cohesion, to add value to its deliberations and to make a difference to its effectiveness. We owe it to ourselves to be as effective as we can by making these vital resources available to the team in the best ways possible. This requires us to be sensitive to the cultures of teams, to the different interpersonal dynamics that are enacted, to the ways that other members are experiencing the teamwork, and to the stresses and tensions that arise from time to time. Like good theatre, effective teamwork is as much about timing, tone of voice, facial expression, gesture and body posture, as it is about clear purposes, elegant ideas, potential solutions and firm decisions.

An important part of personal responsibility in a team is to express our own feelings, to articulate our own difficulties as well as to share our enthusiasms and hopes. We need to be good at enabling the rest of the team to get the best out of us, by appreciating our skills and qualities, recognizing our interests and concerns, and by understanding our difficulties and anxieties. We need to tell the team when we are struggling with frustration, grappling with confusion or bubbling with conviction. Unless we make these aspects of ourselves clear, we should not be surprised if others do not take them into account.

Responsibility to the team

We need to remember that teamwork is a coming together, an enjoining of somewhat disparate skills, energies and commitments. It is often observed that the most effective team members are those who make the most verbal contributions. This is to misunderstand the subtle and beguiling qualities inherent in highly effective collaboration. In order for an individual to make a verbal contribution, others have to be quiet. This can be a passive quietness, waiting for an opportunity to speak. It can also be a dynamic and quiet involvement in which we listen with care and attention to what our colleague is saying. We can be providing encouraging non-verbal support as appropriate, and assessing in our own minds how we might add to and build on the ideas being expressed. Sometimes it is the decision to remain silent that is our most useful contribution. Highly effective teams are superb at active quietness, and success in teamwork depends as much on sacrifice and holding back as it does on rushing in and verbalizing.

Perhaps teamwork and collaboration can only really begin when team members learn to rein in their sometimes errant egos in a striving for team spirit. Our responsibilities to the team need to include the exercising of sacrifice in our own enthusiasms and determinations, but also in acknowledging and appreciating it when we see it being done by others. Responsibility to the team involves a determination to place team success above personal triumph. It is one of the most challenging, but also most rewarding, aspects of human endeavour.

Responsibility to the school

We always need to remember that teams are not an end in themselves, and that they are established to serve organizational needs and aspirations. In teams, we work on behalf of others to make significant contributions to school development and to enrich the lives of all participants. This responsibility is more likely to be exercised when we have a deep sense of our own self-interest, combined with a commitment to team process. In the end, the school will only benefit from the unique contributions of its individual members. The school gains most when in teams, groups and committees there is a powerful synthesizing of individual skills, enthusiasms and commitments.

OPERATIONAL MODES

One of the great challenges of team-focused management is to harness the different skills and qualities of individual team members in a cohesive way. Sometimes teamwork can feel difficult and frustrating because participants seem to be pulling in different directions, competing for speaking time and defending their own positions. This can create confusion, ambiguity and cross-purpose. In order to minimize these time-consuming difficulties, it is necessary for a team to adopt appropriate operational modes. Seven distinctive modes can be considered:

- sharing impressions;
- clarifying information;
- collecting ideas;
- sharing feelings;
- considering options;
- identifying costs and benefits;
- making decisions.

When a team agrees to adopt one of these operational modes, it means that each team member can, for an agreed period of time, deliberately focus his or her thinking in the same direction. This will both increase efficiency and help to avoid the confusions and frustrations caused when team members engage in conflicting modes. Teams which become skilful and disciplined in the choice and use of these modes are likely to require less time than other less disciplined teams to produce higher quality and more consistent task results.

1. *Sharing impressions*. In this mode, team members are dealing with

their initial ideas and reactions to a task or problem, considering the nature of the challenge, the range of subtasks it may require, the knowledge and skills necessary to undertake it, the resources required and the sorts of end results it might demand. Useful questions to focus on in this mode are:

- What is this project about?
- What exactly will the team have to do?
- What ideas and images do particular words or phrases in the task brief evoke?

The main purpose of engaging a team in this mode is to share first impressions and initial reactions. At the beginning of a task when things are not always clear, and people's ideas can be all over the place, it is useful to spend some time in this mode dealing with random thoughts, ideas, questions, confusions and uncertainties. Detailed planning or decision-making should be avoided early on, and energy focused on establishing the impressions of each team member.

It is vital not to inhibit free expression at this stage by pushing for agreement or by attempting to go straight for the right answer. Lateral thinking and the free flow of ideas will help team members to tune in to one another and to the task, and will help to develop team spirit and creativity.

2. *Clarifying information.* This mode provides an opportunity to analyse and clarify information. In order to determine what needs to be done to carry out the project or task, it will be necessary to:

- establish what relevant information the team already has at its disposal; and
- what data and information the team will need to acquire.

It is also important to seek agreement about meanings of key words and phrases in the task brief. Failure to do this early on is likely to create confusion and misunderstanding later, and may in some circumstances jeopardize the quality of the final product. It may also be helpful to use forms to facilitate personal thinking and team discussion (see Fig. 7.2).

The main purpose of this mode is to make sure that common meanings and understandings are established, and that the team has a clear appreciation of the information it has available and that which it will need to acquire.

3. *Collecting ideas.* This mode can be very helpful at any stage of the project cycle. It is aimed at releasing the creativity and imagination of the team. It can be particularly useful early in a task when the team is searching for new angles, possible action steps and effective ways out of tight corners. Later, it can be used when innovation and originality are required, and when it is necessary to come to a decision.

CLARIFYING INFORMATION	
Keypoints for clarification	
Information known	Information needed

Figure 7.2 Clarifying information.

4. *Sharing feelings*. In this mode, team members have the opportunity to deal with the feelings and emotions aroused by the team process. This is a seriously and often dangerously neglected area of management work, but one that is vital to effective collaboration and mutual endeavour. When, for example, energy in the team is low and members are beginning to slump and feel stuck, it is useful to break out of task and go round the team sharing thoughts and feelings. It is important to let everyone have their say without interruption. In one team, such a round produced the following comments:

A: I'm just getting fed up because no-one seems to want to take up my suggestion. I wouldn't mind, but we are constantly getting stuck over this issue and we don't do anything about it.

B: Yes, I notice we always seem to get stuck on this point and I am feeling increasingly annoyed that we haven't followed the agreement we came to in the last process review. Look, we put it up there on the flip chart!

C: Yes, I was feeling frustrated. I feel very angry with myself for not having done anything to remind us about that agreement. I nearly said something five minutes ago but thought I had better not.

D: I'm glad we're now dealing with this. It seemed to me we were going round and round in circles. I'm feeling very stuck. I want us to find some way of moving on so that we finish this session positively and reasonably on target. We're in danger of falling behind schedule.

E: I get really frustrated when we seem to be in reach of an agreement, and then we flounder and get stuck on the same old issue.
We do it time and time again. We should have sorted this out right
at the beginning. I thought we had, but you wouldn't think so
from some of the things being said.

Clearly, there is considerable anger and frustration in the team. Without
this opportunity to deal with these feelings and clear the air, they would
have continued to ferment, further sapping the energy and commitment
of the team. Fortunately, the team has temporarily broken out of task to
deal with this urgent process issue. Going round the team sharing feelings has resulted in the cause of frustration being identified, and allowed
the team to find a solution which will bring it out of its impasse.

5. *Considering options and possibilities*. This mode begins to focus on action.
It responds to such questions as:

• What can we do?
• What choices do we have?
• What are our options?
• What are the alternatives?

In this mode, it is nearly always best to avoid discussion which involves
justifying, promoting or defending particular options or choices. The purpose of the mode is to provide the team with as many options as possible
from which to choose.

6. *Identifying costs and benefits*. This mode moves on a stage from the previous one, presenting opportunities for pros and cons to be considered.
The key question here is: 'What are the costs and benefits of each option?'
It is useful to carry out a cost–benefit analysis of the various options in
order to produce comparative data which can then be related to established boundaries and parameters, as well as to the criteria agreed at the
beginning of the project.

7. *Making decisions*. If the other operational modes have been used
creatively, the making of a decision should not be a difficult or lengthy
process. When faced with a number of options it is best to proceed by
elimination rather than by pushing hard for an immediate winner. Nar-
rowing selection by successively discarding those options that least match
to desired benefits and costs usually facilitates balanced judgement and
effective decision-making.

These distinctive modes offer choices to teams engaged in managing
complex and demanding projects. They are not intended to be adopted
systematically at every stage of project work; rather, they should be
introduced as and when appropriate. A vital part of the skilled management of projects is to engage all team members in the appropriate mode.

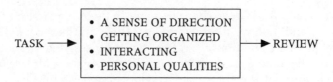

Figure 7.3 Elements of collaboration in teams.

This enables the total energy of the group to be focused rather than fragmented. These seven modes can be applied to most agenda items. Each one has the potential to help a team break out of the undisciplined tradition of open discussion. Workload pressures and time constraints are increasingly requiring us to combine efficiency with effectiveness. To the vital elements of spontaneity, creativity and intuition need to be added the more structured and disciplined procedures of these modes. A team which can happily employ both is likely to meet its deadlines with high-quality results.

TEAM-BUILDING

Team-building is the process of acquiring, applying and developing collaborative skills and qualities within a group of people brought together to manage projects and tasks. Successful teams are created when skilful people come together and are able, through the process of collaboration, to release their skills and qualities to achieve consistently high-quality results. The process of successful collaboration has a number of key elements (see Fig. 7.3).

Task

Without a task there can be little purpose. But in addition to simply stating the job of work that needs to be done, a task provides for a team a set of challenges, offers a range of possibilities and creates a number of opportunities. The team can choose to aim high, and give the task their best effort, or take a minimalist approach to satisfy perceived expectations. Teams which aim low tend to have little self-respect, feel under-challenged by team membership and are unlikely to derive personal and professional satisfaction from working together. In enterprising and high aiming teams, tasks are accepted as voyages of discovery, invitations into the unknown and opportunities for breaking new ground.

Spending time in preparation is the hallmark of an effective and high achieving team. This involves clarifying the task brief, exploring both its explicit requirements and its implicit meanings, and striving to achieve a shared perception of the job in hand.

A sense of direction

Good teams know where they are going. They spend time sorting out intentions and clarifying purposes and end results. They work hard to create in the mind of each team member a strong visual image of what they want to end up with. This not only reinforces intention, it minimizes the possibility of ending up with something that nobody wanted.

Getting organized

This involves constant attention to process and procedure. Experimenting and refining systematic frameworks and modifying rules and procedures all combine to increase efficiency through shared understanding. Awareness of the time element means that expectations are set realistically, within the resources available.

Above all, getting organized means harnessing and activating the skills present within the team. It is useful to note four aspects:

- *Understanding*: knowing what to do.
- *Skill*: being able to do it.
- *Commitment*: wanting to do it.
- *Application*: actually doing it.

Interactions

Good teams are those in which team members demonstrate communication skills at a high level. The important interpersonal skills in teamwork include:

- thinking;
- listening;
- handling ideas;
- supporting other team members;
- providing encouragement;
- sharing feelings;
- self-discipline – resisting the temptation to take up air time without a really good reason.

There is sometimes a tendency to assume that those who make the most verbal contributions in a team are the most useful and effective team members. It is also important to recognize that not airing a view or stating a position is also making a vital contribution. Many contributions offered in task teams are either destructive (i.e. they attack the positions of others, producing ill feeling and a reduction in commitment) or delaying (i.e. they take attention away from consideration of important issues). The issue of hidden agendas is often raised as a barrier to effective teamwork. It is hopeless to try and avoid them, and the best strategy is to make them explicit and acceptable – get them on the table.

Personal qualities

This involves behaving in ways that are comfortable with other colleagues – being open and honest, speaking directly, appreciating the efforts of others and being aware that effective behaviour is a matter of choice not accident. In good teams, there is a determination to encourage the release of personal qualities to the team. This is best facilitated by providing specific success feedback to team members both at the time and in process reviews. Team members grow in confidence when their skilful contributions are well received, but they can only build on these successes if the feedback they receive is factual, specific and detailed.

Review

Improving the quality of teamwork involves a commitment to deliberate learning through experience. Reviewing is the process of submitting experience to analysis so that the processes of collaboration can be more powerfully understood. What we learn through reviewing enables us to build on successful practice and to eliminate or change what does not work. The following agenda for process development provides a useful checklist for review:

1 In what specific ways can we ensure that we have a shared understanding of the task the team is faced with?
2 What practical steps can we take to ensure that the team has established clear purposes and end results for the task?
3 What shall we do to create structures and frameworks to guide the efficient management of the task?
4 How shall we give attention to developing interpersonal communication in the team and dealing with hidden agendas?
5 In what practical ways can we create opportunities to offer and receive feedback on our contributions?
6 How can we ensure that process reviews become a fixed and regular part of the team-building process?

DEVELOPING THE MANAGEMENT STRUCTURE

One of the great challenges facing a primary school determined to build a management culture based on staff involvement and collaboration, is the need to abandon some deeply entrenched positions.

Competition

Throughout our childhoods and schooling, and later in the organizations which employ us, we are socialized into a competitive ethic. Being smarter than someone else, getting better grades, living in a better area and receiving a higher salary have become synonymous with success and achievement. Cooperation has not been high on the agenda of qualities to develop in schools and workplaces, and it is not surprising that so many of us find it difficult, often preferring to work on our own.

Hierarchy

In organizations, hierarchies have been developed to emphasize vertical separation and steep career ladders. It is important to be aware of the effects that separating colleagues in such a way can have (see Chapter 5). Status and salary differentials have traditionally been the cause of a great deal of discontent and conflict, and the tendency in recent years has been to produce flatter organizations with fewer status levels.

People at the top of hierarchies tend to see their roles as interesting, challenging, unpredictable and satisfying. They have the opportunity to bring to their work the whole gamut of experience and expertise. On the other hand, people low down or at the bottom of hierarchies, tend to feel bored and fatalistic, hemmed in and frustrated because so little of their total repertoire of skills and experience is involved in their work. Oppressive hierarchies tend to diminish people, make them less than they usually are and certainly less than they could be. Such a crushing of human enterprise is bad for the organization, ensuring a poorer quality of product or service than is possible.

Individualism

In schools, the professionalism of teachers has been built on an assumption of autonomy of practice. While the content of what is to be learnt by pupils is laid down in national and school policies, the ways in which teachers organize and manage that learning is largely a matter of personal choice. In addition, as extra management responsibilities have become an increasing part of the professional work of teachers, there has been a tendency to create management roles that emphasize individualism and personal accountability.

In recent years, teachers in primary schools have demonstrated their considerable capacities for cooperation and collaboration through their handling of endless change projects. What has been remarkable has been the speed and thoroughness with which schools have accomplished multiple innovation. This has not been achieved without cost, and many teachers have paid a high price for the enormous effort and commitment they have given to their work.

Much of this success has been achieved through what can be described as cooperative individualism – individual teachers pursuing single and often lonely curriculum leadership roles, but within a caring and supportive staff culture. It is now time to break out of this disparate process and bring staff together in the sort of task-focused partnerships and small project teams outlined in this and previous chapters. The evolutionary crisis has highlighted the limits of individualism. The future will be built on collaboration.

8 ◆ TRANSFORMATIVE LEADERSHIP

Over the past twenty-five years or so, we have seen a steady development in the management structure of primary schools, with curriculum coordinators playing an increasingly important role. In the future it will be the leadership aspect of all managerial roles that will determine the capacity of primary schools to develop the confidence that will enable them to survive the evolutionary crisis. When leaders succumb to increased pressures, faster change, heightened confusion and greater complexity, then both direction and energy can be sacrificed. In these days of stress, uncertainty and frustration, people don't want to be managed, they want to be led. Organizations, and perhaps our nation as well, are craving leadership which will create the conditions in which the best we have to offer can effectively be harnessed in the face of difficulties and obstacles. There is vital transformational work to be done by those who can exercise leadership in all our institutions and organizations.

CONCEPTS OF LEADERSHIP

We have inherited a set of ideas and beliefs about leadership which will be hard to change. The tradition of command and control that held nations and societies in its grip, worked well when the majority of the followers had little access to information and expertise, but we have seen what happened in the former Soviet Union when it was no longer possible to keep things secret. Leadership of the informed and educated has to be different, and it is only slowly dawning on western societies that effective and necessary action will only follow if leadership flows through collaboration, consultation and consensus. In organizations where information flows freely, then larger proportions of people want to be involved in decision-making. We have seen the democratic structures of political parties, trades unions and voluntary organizations change to accommodate participative structures as well as representational ones.

Autocracies are breaking down and decision-making proceeds less through the issuing of orders than the development of a shared sense of direction among those who will be required to pursue it. Leadership becomes less the activity of named officials and more a process of dynamic improvisation, involving people at all levels of organizational life. Our traditional reliance on hierarchy is under threat, and it will become increasingly difficult for those set on the command and control course to sustain the disempowerment of individuals that inevitably accompanies it. Hierarchy is more concerned with location than with action, with where people are in the status league than with what they are currently working on. All staff need to be project leaders and to have significant opportunities to release skills and qualities that traditional structures would have crushed and inhibited.

One way to assist the development of a new paradigm for organizational management is to redefine the terms we use. Because of our education and upbringing, and indeed our daily engagement with national and international news, we tend to equate leadership with leaders – those in powerful positions in international and institutional affairs. For those concerned to help in the development of effective leadership, this has tended to create problems of definition. We have a tendency to think of leadership in terms of role and personality; that is, leadership can only be considered as a function of those who occupy top positions in particular institutions and organizations. This suggests that leadership can only be practised if one is given a position of power and authority from which to act. Certainly many of those occupying such positions do demonstrate characteristics of leadership, but there are dangers in attributing such behaviour only to those so highly placed, and extending the assumption to the idea that only those so placed are able to exercise it.

Theorists have approached the issue of leadership from many angles. A common one is to take a dozen or so outstanding leaders (by common perception) and attempt to extrapolate the characteristics they seem to have in common. This results in a list of 'power behaviours' which seem to contain the clues to success. There is little evidence to suggest that this is effective in leadership training. Another false avenue is to try and tease out what it is in the personality and experience of successful leaders that may serve to explain their skills, abilities and qualities.

A more productive avenue is to ask the following question: What is it that enables successful organizations to succeed and thrive? What emerges is a more complex answer than simply good leadership from the top. It seems that leadership is an altogether more diffuse concept than we have traditionally come to believe, that it can be exercised at all levels within organizations, and that all participants are capable of practising it in some way. By focusing only on the behaviour of senior people, we run the risk of losing sight of those aspects of human behaviour in organizations that lead to effectiveness and high quality.

One useful definition of leadership is as follows: 'Behaviour that enables and assists others to achieve personal and organizational ambitions and goals'. This suggests that leadership might have as much to do with making helpful suggestions as to issuing strategic directives, as much about listening to other people's ideas as to expounding one's own, and as much about gentleness as about toughness. What is clear is that effectiveness in organizations depends upon leadership emerging appropriately as and when necessary. Perhaps we need to change the question from 'Who are good leaders?' to 'What examples have you seen of colleagues demonstrating good leadership?'. It will only be when we observe qualities of leadership in our daughters and sons, in the new and youngest recruits to our organizations and in the pupils that we teach, that we will really begin to appreciate how limiting our traditional view has been.

Taking the definition a stage further, we can propose an altogether more life-enhancing concept: 'Leadership is helping people to be as effective as (a) they themselves want to be and (b) they have the potential to be'. We need to let go of the inherited belief that leadership is about making people what they are not. Too many leaders are plagued with the unreasonable expectations raised on their own role, that they seem to have no choice but to do the same to their colleagues. Leadership which flows from this more life-enhancing definition has some important features:

1 Leadership needs to be seen as a function of a group rather than the role of an individual.
2 Leadership can be behaviour which gives power away.
3 The aims of leadership should be an increase in self-directedness and the release of energy, imagination and creativity in all those who form the organization.
4 Leadership is behaviour which energizes, activates and increases the capacity of individuals and groups to move ever nearer to shared visions and aims.
5 Leadership behaviour is best designed by the followers. Leaders need to seek information from their colleagues about the sort of leadership that suits them best.
6 One of the key functions of leadership is to help in the creation of conditions in which people feel motivated to work to the optimum levels of their energy, interest and commitment.

In moving towards more life-enhancing leadership, we need to question our very assumptions about people and personal power. This new concept of leadership adopts an approach which recognizes that the potential and power to work effectively lies within the person, rather than in the leader. We still cling on to assumptions that the nature of people is such that they cannot be trusted to direct their own work, and that they must be instructed, guided, monitored, controlled, rewarded and punished. Life-centred leaders believe in the basic dignity and worth of people, and in their capacity for commitment, self-direction and achievement. The effectiveness of a leader is not always in what they give to us, but what they refuse to take away – our self-respect, our integrity and our potential to make a significant contribution.

For leaders, this involves having the strength to permit others to be themselves, to honour those ideas and values which may not be identical to their own. Carl Rogers (1978) observed that it can be a real test of leadership to do this, to struggle to let others be themselves, and to allow them to develop in ways which are uniquely their own. It is in this basic attitude to others that the secrets of effective leadership lie. The essence of this attitude is that of valuing and trusting the essential self of each individual in the team. If such a stance is adopted, then the potential of team members will be more readily released. Rogers further observes that leadership is not effective when:

> . . . I have tried to create in another individual something that is not already there; I have found, however, that if I can provide the conditions that allow growth to occur, then this positive directional tendency brings about constructive results.
>
> (Rogers 1980: 120)

All of this poses a further dilemma about whether leaders should strive to provide the leadership which their colleagues need if they are to succeed, or whether to provide the leadership they think their colleagues ought to have. Leaders, too, have to be themselves, and the worst kind of leadership is often created when individual leaders work to obey imposed or inherited strictures about what they think they should do.

For most people, the idea of a really exciting job is the one they seek, rather than the one they are currently doing. Leadership is the process of helping people to make their present job as exciting, interesting and as absorbing as possible, so that they will bring to it all those skills and qualities they seem to be keeping in store for the job they hope to get.

LEADERSHIP AND PRIMARY SCHOOLS

Primary schools are leadership-intensive organizations. All members of the teaching staff have significant leadership roles, most running their own organizations of thirty or so pupils. Simultaneously, they carry whole-school responsibilities for subject coordination and other functions. The smaller the school, the larger the range of responsibilities. While staff may be payed on a differential scale, primary schools have seldom placed an over-heavy emphasis on hierarchical distinctions, although headteachers have traditionally performed a range of functions different from their colleagues. Recent years have seen the adoption of senior management teams, spreading the increasing management workload between senior colleagues and widening the base for decision-making. There has, however, been some reluctance to recognize the leadership potential of all professional staff, and management responsibility has been seen only in terms of work done beyond the classroom. One of the most unique features of primary school teaching is the taking on of significant organizational leadership so early in a career. All the skills and qualities necessary for the leadership of other types of organizations are required to bring about successful learning among thirty children in the collective setting of the classroom.

Primary schools have the potential to become genuine heterarchical organizations, reconfiguring the management structure according to the tasks in hand. When a subject development task is the focus for collaborative work, then that subject leader assumes the most senior responsibility. All staff at some time are in this position. We need to recognize the inherent flexibility of this approach to leadership, and recognize that in primary schools leadership is a function of the whole team and not the role of one individual. Roland Barth (1988) has coined the phrase 'a community of leaders' to capture the potential for shared leadership in primary schools. He contends that nowadays schools need more leadership than the headteacher has time for, and makes the following propositions:

- All teachers have leadership tendencies.
- Schools badly need teacher leadership.
- Teacher leadership has not been forthcoming.
- Headteacher leadership has been too pivotal.

This suggests that the leadership structure of primary schools has considerable potential for development. One way to achieve this would be to move from a structure based on functions and individuals to one built on tasks, projects and teams. The effective school will be the one that has designed its leadership with needs-responsive flexibility in mind. In most primary schools, leadership roles are allocated to staff on an individual and long-term basis, so that each member of staff, in addition to class-teaching responsibilities, carries a curriculum coordination portfolio for the foreseeable future. This means that curriculum leadership is carried out by individuals often working alone and separated from their colleagues. There is good sense in this model: expertise can be developed and shared, and there tends to be continuity. However there are also disadvantages. Working alone developing policy statements, attempting to monitor operations and keeping abreast of subject developments can be lonely, time-consuming work, often at odds with the demands of the class-teaching role. What happens in practice is that each subject leader works as best they can in relation to the school development plan and according to the demands of their job description.

In their study of roles and responsibilities in primary schools, Rosemary Webb and Graham Vulliamy (1996) provide a range of valuable information about subject coordination and point to three particular constraints on the role:

1 The problem of expertise.
2 Lack of time for coordination tasks.
3 The nature of power relationships within the primary school.

Not only do these constraints highlight the limitations of the individualistic approach outlined in Chapter 7, they emphasize the need to harness experience and expertise in more imaginative ways. If there is a problem with sustaining the epithet 'expert', why do we not abolish it and adopt the notion of 'specialist'? This assumes a commitment of interest and concern in a curriculum area, rather than an assumption of superiority. Curriculum coordination should be about helping and supporting colleagues, not being in competition with them.

A more fluid and flexible approach makes the school development plan the basis of the leadership structure. If the plan envisages four specific pieces of curriculum development for the year ahead, then the leadership structure needs to be designed with that plan in mind. Four project teams can be created, each with a clear brief to manage the project on behalf of the staff as a whole. Such projects could run consecutively or concurrently. The advantages of this team-focused project approach is to get work done more quickly and efficiently, and to harness the skills and qualities of all staff more equally.

Figure 8.1 shows the leadership structure of a one-form entry primary school with eight members of staff. The school development plan has established four development projects together with a review task and a community development initiative. In this particular structure, the head (A) provides support and encouragement to all projects, takes an active part in two, but not in the chairing role. The deputy head (B) works in three teams, as does the senior allowance holder (C). All other colleagues work in two teams, apart from (H), who is newly qualified and recently appointed. This particular configuration is temporary. When a project is completed, there is a planned gap before a new one is taken up, but individuals are available to join the *ad hoc* team, which can be convened when urgent and unexpected tasks arise.

Some tasks in a typical school development plan may be quite short-lived, perhaps occupying a small task team for a week or two. Others may be more substantial, ranging over a whole academic year and involving some change of team membership as the project develops. Through

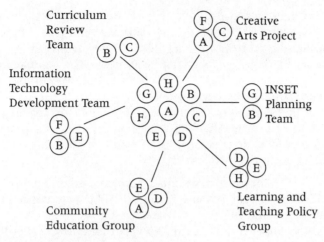

Figure 8.1 Team-focused leadership.

the regular pattern of staff meetings, teams refer to the staff as a whole, making periodic reports and receiving recommendations, observations, responses and suggestions.

Within the projects teams, status differentials can be minimized, and each member of staff encouraged to contribute according to their experience and skill. There are many benefits to be accrued from such a dynamic and highly participative structure:

- it maximizes staff expertise and experience;
- it involves all staff in key management and leadership activities;
- it achieves a higher work rate;
- it removes the frustrations often experienced when decision-making is attempted in too large a group;
- it develops new skills and expertise;
- it facilitates professional development;
- it increases enjoyment and commitment;
- it makes better use of time;
- it allows quicker responses to new problems.

Perhaps more than anything, this sort of approach to shared leadership helps a school to move from a red light mentality – restricting access to action and development – to a green light mentality – encouraging easy access and involvement in the key tasks of school development. Devolving authority to the task and its team will release heads from too detailed an involvement in development and change, and allow the fuller expression of staff talent and ambition. Teams should be encouraged to set their own detailed targets within the brief designed by the staff as a whole.

In his fascinating and detailed analysis of primary school headship, Geoff Southworth (1995) notes how traditional and recent bureaucratic regulation has driven heads into a sort of chief executive role, inhibiting their capacity to provide educational leadership. The approach outlined above, and discussed in Chapter 7, could offer one way to halt this dangerous trend. Southworth also suggests that notions of social justice need to be the foundation upon which primary school management structures are built. He notes that the micropolitics of school management can have a considerable effect on children and wonders how schools can create model authority structures:

> For too long, I believe we have underestimated, or underemphasized, the political potency of schools. There is a hidden (or not so hidden) political curriculum in schools. It teaches pupils about: hierarchical organization; super-ordinates exercising authority over subordinates; power and knowledge flowing downwards – from the top; whose voices count and whose are unheard and suppressed. The central issue, and an important outcome, for me, is the need to recognize the moral and political potency of schools and their impact on young children.
>
> (Southworth 1995: 218)

ROLE DEFINITIONS AND JOB DESCRIPTIONS

A more democratic, egalitarian and supportive approach to leadership demands new thinking on job descriptions and role definitions. Far too often job descriptions for management roles, such as curriculum coordination, are couched in 'eternal' terms referring to quite general areas of activity for many years to come. They usually define areas of responsibility, rather than tasks to be managed. Such job descriptions can create considerable difficulties:

- They tend to encourage rigidity: 'It's not my job'.
- They stifle initiative, when what is required is flexibility and enterprise.
- They tend to define professional activity, rather than inspire energy and imagination.

Flexible leadership in primary schools will need more imaginative and motivating job descriptions. In one school, after a period of considerable struggle for tighter and tighter definitions of role, the staff realized that the secret lay in freedom rather than description, and came up with a small post-it sized statement for everyone consisting of only three words – DO YOUR BEST! It was the trusting assumption behind this that the staff found so invigorating, encouraging them to see beyond the somewhat pedestrian demands of their traditional and often restrictive job definitions.

In considering how job descriptions might be devised to help in the creation of the sorts of interesting and stimulating jobs most of us want, it is useful to consider the following, all of which have featured in some radical examples of primary school job descriptions:

- Enjoy your work.
- Pursue your interests and enthusiasms.
- Connect with colleagues constantly.
- Announce all successes and achievements.
- Keep asking questions.
- Allocate time for thinking and reflection.
- Take some risks.
- Have a dream that we can all buy into.

In determining the membership of projects teams, one school has developed the following criteria:

- How can we make this project special?
- What can we learn from it?
- How can we have fun with it?

In defining leadership roles and responsibilities, there are a number of ways in which whole-staff involvement can be harnessed:

1 Set up a development project on team-focused leadership, job descriptions and appropriate management training. Plan a pilot project and report back on options for action.
2 Circulate everyone's job descriptions to all members of staff with the request: 'How can this job help you to carry out your own role more effectively?'
3 Send a memo to colleagues asking, 'In my specialist area, what particular sorts of help will be of most support to you?'
4 Plan an INSET day on issues of leadership and support. Invite an external facilitator so all members of staff can participate fully.
5 Plan a short course on leadership skills for pupils. Run it as an optional activity and find out what the children think of leadership, and what sort they like best.

In working to create more imaginative role definitions for those taking on leadership work in primary schools, it is useful to identify the wide-ranging nature of leadership work. Figure 8.2 illustrates two distinct ways in which leaders operate. The *managerial* roles refer to those parts of leadership which are concerned with providing leadership for the whole school as in the work of the headteacher, or in providing leadership for a particular project in the case of a curriculum coordinator. In this mode, the leader is concerned to help colleagues in particular ways:

Managerial
modes

- Conceptual
- Directional
- Structural
- Cultural
- Transitional

Interactive
modes

- Informative
- Explorative
- Active
- Authoritative
- Reflective

Figure 8.2   Leadership modes.

- *Conceptual*: working with ideas, concepts, models and frameworks.
- *Directional*: articulating and clarifying visions, policies and plans.
- *Structural*: creating systems and procedures to facilitate action.
- *Cultural*: building the psychological climate to promote interest, excitement, commitment and fun.
- *Transitional*: assisting the process of change through encouragement and support.

In the *interactive* mode, face to face with individuals, groups or teams, the leader works through interpersonal communication:

- *Informative*: providing data, supplying documentation, creating access to resources.
- *Explorative*: confronting problems, considering options and choices, building scenarios, anticipating consequences, estimating costs and benefits.
- *Active*: working alongside colleagues as an equal team member.
- *Authoritative*: defining boundaries, taking decisions, spreading authority down the organization.
- *Reflective*: pausing to think, reviewing progress to date, taking stock, drawing conclusions.

The skill lies in slipping into the mode appropriate to the situation and being able to adapt in the spontaneity of the moment to the constantly shifting needs of individuals and teams. This is exciting work, very similar to that used by classroom teachers in the management of learning.

THE INTERPERSONAL WORLD

Table 8.1 makes a distinction between the old paradigm imperative of leadership (i.e. power and control) and the new paradigm leadership principle of influence and support. It is through these interpersonal transactions that the real work of leadership is done. Many of these arise in the form of interruptions to planned activities and they can create a sense of frustration that our time is being eroded and we can begin to feel irritated that we don't seem to be able to control our professional

Table 8.1 The shifting paradigm

Old paradigm leadership (power and control)	New paradigm leadership (influence and support)
Leader behaviour	*Leader behaviour*
Makes decisions	Gives authority to others
Gives orders	Frees people to do 'their own thing'
Directs behaviour	Expresses own ideas and feelings
Exercises authority over others	Stimulates independence of thought and action
Coerces and cajoles	Encourages and supports
Instructs and supervises	Seeks information on progress and provides feedback on success
Evaluates others	Encourages self-review and self-evaluation
Gives rewards and punishments	Helps others to celebrate successes and confront difficulties

life. Interruptions are the expression of temporary but real frustrations with other people's work. If the frustration or need is not dealt with, then quality of work suffers. It is interesting to conceive of leadership as a series of encounters with the unexpected, turning our skills and qualities to what happens in the moment-to-moment challenges of organizational life. It is in these spontaneous moments that headteachers, deputies, curriculum coordinators and classroom teachers do some of their very best work. We have to learn that interruptions are not unfair demands upon our time, but opportunities to shine, to offer ourselves to the needs of others, and to recognize that leadership is a supply process and not a requirement exercise.

One of the worrying trends in recent years has been the pressure on heads to preside over increasingly complex bureaucratic procedures. This takes them away from the real work of school development. In a recent study of leadership characteristics, Tom Peters (1992) noted that those leaders who make the biggest impact on helping their colleagues to be effective:

- are available all the time;
- rarely sit down in the office;
- apply energy to encouraging others;
- constantly encourage colleagues to be imaginative and creative;
- always enquire into how things are going, taking a real interest in detail but not getting too involved;
- greet and meet people as they come and go;
- walk around the organization three or four times a day.

It is how we behave in the many face-to-face situations of school life that determines whether we influence and support pupils and colleagues effectively. David Howe (1993) suggests that much depends on our capacity to be more aware of, and to respond to, three basic needs in others: the need to feel accepted, the need to feel acknowledged and the need to feel entitled.

- *Feeling accepted*: leaders can help us to feel part of the past, present and future of the school. They can help us to believe that we have an important part to play in the scheme of things, and that our contribution is significant and special.
- *Feeling acknowledged*: leaders can notice us. They can draw attention to those parts of our work which interest and delight them. They can provide encouraging feedback and also draw our achievements to the attention of others.
- *Feeling entitled*: leaders can help us to feel that it is okay to be who we are, to have the feelings we experience, and to hold the beliefs that are important to us.

The effect of these leadership behaviours is to affirm our self-esteem, to help us to feel worthwhile, both about ourselves and about our contribution to the development of the school. Central to this is the capacity of leaders to understand their colleagues and to engage with them in the struggle to achieve what is important to them in their lives. Geoffrey Bellman (1990) suggests that it is the very process of taking an interest in what is important to us that has such a powerful effect on our professional energy and commitment. Leaders, he says, can really make an impact by:

- Helping others to figure out what they would be proudest of doing in their role, and helping them to do it.
- Helping them to satisfy important personal goals through their professional role.
- Helping them to clarify and empower medium- and long-term ambitions.
- Helping them to search for, and discover, meaning in the daily grind.
- Helping them to activate and honour the small voice deep inside them which seeks expression and understanding.
- Helping them to become who they really want to be.

As we discover more and more about those behaviours which seem to make a significant difference in enabling others to release and express more of their potential, the more we will see leadership as a process of human nourishment and less a matter of keeping people to their contracts. John Rowan (1992) points to the subtlety of many of these interpersonal processes. He suggests that helping others to be effective involves what he calls 'unhindering', supporting the removal of blocks that people often put in the way of their own development. Development also involves the process of 'unfolding', encouraging others to allow what is deep within themselves to come to the surface of their being rather than to lay hidden and concealed.

Rowan (1992) also reminds us that Abraham Maslow (1978) observed that at every moment in our lives we have a choice between the joys of safety and the joys of growth. Far too often in the troubled and conflictual cultures of many organizations, we choose the safety option, thereby denying ourselves the possibility of development and growth, but also preventing our skills and qualities from having a greater impact on the organization itself. Perhaps the very heart of leadership is helping people to *do justice to their own potential*.

Surviving the evolutionary crisis will require us to dig deeper into our reservoirs of locked and trapped potential, and of developing approaches to leadership which are enabling and supportive. Leadership is important to help others to avoid the terrifying prospect which Maslow (1978: 35) warned us of: 'If you deliberately plan to be less than you are capable of being, then I warn you that you will be deeply unhappy for the rest of your life. You will be evading your possibilities'.

One of the ways into this challenging future is to acknowledge that in primary schools we are all in the leadership business. Children are learning about it all the time, and exercising it in relation to the management of their own learning as well as with their friends and family. The leadership behaviours described in this chapter are very much the ones good teachers employ with their pupils. Curriculum coordinators provide support and encouragement for colleagues in specific areas of the learning programme, and heads and deputies use leadership to support and encourage colleagues in their challenging roles. Since we are all in the leadership business, we should perhaps spend more time thinking and talking about it. The following questions raise some fundamental issues about how leadership is conceived and practised (Jeffers 1992):

- In what ways is this organization helping me to satisfy my ambitions and aspirations for my life and work?
- In what ways is this organization helping me to participate in the direction and development of its present and future?
- In what ways is this organization helping me to contribute to the welfare and well-being of society?
- In what ways is this organization helping me to lay healthy foundations and opportunities for future generations?

Engaging with these questions on a school INSET day would certainly open up rich avenues for exploration, and create some very powerful agendas for school development.

In considering the spontaneous nature of much leadership work, Gareth Morgan (1993) suggests some characteristic features of successful leaders:

- They have clear and passionate aspirations.
- They don't *force fit* their vision, or direct and cajole to enforce it.
- They manage in open-ended ways – encouraging and allowing desirable initiatives to emerge from evolving situations.
- They are opportunistic in their approach to change.
- They build on ideas, actions and events which they initiate, or which spontaneously come their way.
- They are strategic, in the sense that, while they rely on spontaneity and the haphazardness of events, they are always guided by a strong sense of vision – of what they are ultimately trying to achieve.
- They know where they want to go, but don't always know the route by which they are going to get there.

It is through the countless interpersonal transactions of the school day that people's lives are changed, organizational improvements are made, dreams are realized and needs are met. We need more understanding of the complex psychological dynamics of those snatched moments in corridors. While we cannot plan for these unexpected incidents, we can be prepared for them, appreciating that they present golden opportunities to encourage and support. It is not so much a matter of what is said in these moments, as what our basic stance in these transactions consists of. David Howe (1993) suggests that three ingredients need to be present if the relationship is to work effectively:

- *Acceptance*: the creation of a secure emotional base to the transaction.
- *Understanding*: an appreciation and sensitivity to the felt experience of the other person.
- *Dialogue*: the communication of meaning and understanding.

These contrast very vividly with the leadership toxins that Senge (1990) describes. He suggests that leaders are at their most ineffective when:

1 They try too hard to get people committed.
2 They set the direction for others.
3 They alone make the key decisions.
4 They sustain a traditional view of leadership based on:
   (a) assumptions of people's powerlessness;
   (b) their lack of personal vision;
   (c) the presence of faults which have to be remedied.

Life-centred leadership is essentially a catalytic process, helping others to bring about changes in themselves. Catalytic energy is supplied to the other person who has the potential for effective action, but that potentiality is not yet activated. Through dialogue with the leader, that potential energy is activated and transformed into kinetic energy. This catalytic

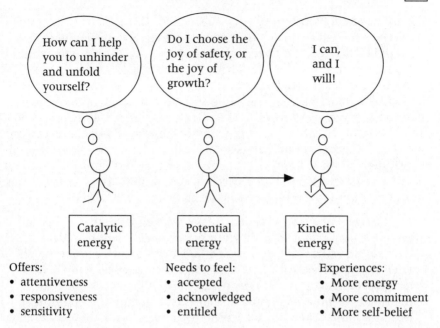

Figure 8.3 Catalytic leadership.

capacity is created when a complex combination of attitudes, stances and interpersonal skills crystallize within the transaction. Howe (1993) emphasizes the importance of the stances we take in these situations and highlights three:

- *Attentiveness*: offering undivided attention in a warm and caring way, and showing a real interest in the other's concerns.
- *Responsiveness*: verbal and non-verbal responding which conveys understanding and which helps the other person to solve their own problems and make their own decisions.
- *Sensitivity*: demonstrating a caring acceptance of the other person's feelings in the situation.

Figure 8.3 attempts to capture some of the elements of this complex process.

TRANSFORMING LEADERSHIP

The process of transforming leadership in primary schools will not be easy. It will involve, for many of us, the giving up of lifetime habits and practices, and being prepared to submit all traditional precepts and beliefs to the most rigorous re-examination. Generations of accumulated assumptions which have hugely underestimated the potential of both children and adults will need to be challenged. Those management practices which tend to crush and confine, rather than liberate and unfold, will need to be changed. We have to prepare to create entirely new maps to navigate our journey into the future.

We have to dig much deeper into our powerful reservoirs of creativity and imagination, and combine as never before in alliances of collaboration to chart our ways through the stormy seas ahead. Primary schools are especially well placed to engage in this transformational process, but the work of leaders in primary schools will not be for the faint-hearted. It will depend on strong constitutions, dearly held visions of what can be achieved, bold ambitions and courageous action. The nature of this transformation is well captured by Peter Senge (1990: 359):

> Most of the outstanding leaders I have worked with are neither tall nor especially handsome; they are often mediocre public speakers; they do not stand out in a crowd and they do not mesmerise an attending audience with their brilliance or eloquence. Rather, what distinguishes them is the clarity and persuasiveness of their ideas, the depth of their commitment and their openness to continually learning more. They do not have 'the answer'. But they do instil confidence in those around them that, together 'we can learn whatever we need to learn in order to achieve the results we truly desire'.
>
> The ability of such people to be natural leaders, as near as I can tell, is the by-product of a lifetime of effort to develop conceptual and communication skills, to reflect on personal values and to align personal behaviour with values, to learn how to listen and to appreciate others and others' ideas. In the absence of such effort, personal charisma is a style without substance. It leaves those affected less able to think for themselves and less able to make wise choices. It can devastate an organization or society.

Perhaps what is most exciting in the future for primary schools is to build enough confidence to restore the pioneering and innovative tradition which has been so ruthlessly derided in recent years. The life-centred approach to learning outlined in Chapter 4 requires life-centred leadership and management. Southworth's (1995) suggestion that we need to develop approaches to school management and leadership which provide powerful learning models of authority structures for pupils is a big idea which we should place right at the heart of our developmental agenda. Such a vision for primary schools requires that we not only widen the management process to all staff, but to pupils as well, enabling them to become active co-managers of the learning process. Some schools are well on the way. In the years ahead, the paradigm shift will continue, and primary schools will have a significant part to play in our society's journey to more life-enhancing organizations and institutions.

9 ▶ MEETING THE FUTURE

THE EVOLUTIONARY CHALLENGE

One of the main themes of this book has been the idea that many of the structures and processes that have sustained educational development since the beginning of this century may no longer be appropriate to the changed and continuously changing circumstances of the next. A continuation of the tinkering reforms to the education system in recent years will not be sufficient to satisfy the increasingly desperate expectations raised on it. In the evolutionary crisis facing our institutions and organizations, radical departures from tradition are called for if we are to survive. In his study of the volatile and turbulent conditions in which we now find ourselves, Gareth Morgan (1988: xii) notes that managers and their organizations are facing wave upon wave of change and that they need both to accept this as a new reality and rise to its many challenges:

> This will require an approach to management and the development of managerial competence that is proactive and future oriented, so that future challenges will be tackled with foresight and flexibility, and managers and their organizations will be able to deal with the opportunities created by change, rather than allow the waves to sweep over them.

The struggles of the education service to adapt to the novel and unprecedented challenges arising out of the changed and continuously changing nature of education and society, will need to be supported by a wider framework of ideas and strategies than are currently employed. New insights, approaches and practices are needed to produce a more substantial theoretical and practical foundation for the effective management of schools as we move into the twenty-first century.

We are currently witnessing increasing confusion about how the management of work is conducted. The growing amounts of pressure,

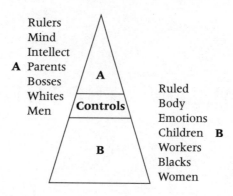

Figure 9.1 Hierarchies of power and control.

frustration, guilt and dysfunction being experienced in the organizations of our society, are perhaps a cry for new processes and new systems. It is as if we are at last rising to challenge one of the key principles upon which the whole idea of organization has been built – that people, and how they are treated, is one of the least significant factors for consideration. We have obediently complied with the tyranny of hierarchy, with its assumption that only the people at the top are capable of making decisions and taking responsibility and that people lower down in hierarchies are naturally inferior in all aspects of human endeavour, and are by and large happy to accept this in-built inferiority.

Organizations are essentially political institutions concerned with power. John Rowan (1983) suggested that our obsession with hierarchical structures reflects a dualistic conception of the world, where one part is supposed to control another part. He illustrated this through a simple diagram (see Fig. 9.1). The reason, Rowan argued, that A has to control B, is that A is afraid of B. So A behaves in ways which reinforce B's conformity to authority, denying them power, emphasizing conformity of behaviour and regulating standards of performance. For A, the danger is that the lower groups might break through and overwhelm them, jeopardizing all the benefits and advantages they have accrued.

In challenging these entrenched patterns and attempting to find ways out of this dualistic trap, we have to envisage a redistribution of authority and power. Revolutionary theory has often seen the process of overthrow where A is kicked out and replaced by B. Perhaps we need to see it in more organic and integrative terms, where A stands to gain benefit from such a redistribution. What is so abusive about organizational hierarchies is the appalling waste of human talent they preside over.

Writing ten years after this analysis, Rowan (1992) looks to a more humanistic solution to the crisis in which we set about systematically encouraging the development of human potential. This involves, he suggests, questioning all those structures (whether internal or external) that limit and constrain people:

> The main internal constraint seems to be rigid patterns of thought and action that have been set up as answers to the problems of living; however effective these may have been at the time they were first used, they have now turned into handcuffs or blinkers that prevent movement or awareness.
>
> (Rowan 1992: 63)

It is through more sensitive and caring relationships, and by adopting more life-centred teaching and management behaviours, that these patterns can be questioned in ways which encourage personal and professional change. In the process, argues Rowan, damaged and crushed self-images can be dismantled, and:

> . . . the rich realm of subjectivity that was pushed down as too dangerous and too weak is now opened up and entered into and allowed to exist and be used and transformed. There is a feeling of being real instead of unreal.
>
> (Rowan 1992: 63)

The main external constraints, he suggests, are rigid social patterns that have been set up as answers to the problems of living. However effective they may have been in the past:

> These have now turned into hobbles and straitjackets that prevent change or awareness. Through the process of consciousness raising, organizational work, social research and political activism, these patterns are questioned in such a way that they can start to move.
>
> (Rowan 1992: 63)

One of the keys to the shifting of this inhibiting paradigm of human organization is to replace the traditional reliance on power and control with a new emphasis on learning and exploration. This process is not about learning a set of fixed answers, argues Rowan, but learning as a continuous process of coming to know. This is what transforms control into a process of co-creation, where we genuinely take responsibility for our world.

This requires a new concern for vulnerability, a quality often experienced in organizations, but rarely attended to. We cannot learn much, according to Rowan, when all our defences are up:

> It is the horror, and the shame of the world we live in that so often we seem driven to defend ourselves, forced to raise our barriers. It takes real inner strength, and staunch allies, to keep on going for a better world.
>
> (Rowan 1992: 64)

Meeting such challenging demands will require the creation of new maps and models. Charles Handy (1994), discussing how we can make sense of the future, notes that the acceptance of paradox in our lives is the first step towards living and managing with it. He notes the potential for disorder as traditional structures fragment and disintegrate, but points to the work of scientists working with complexity theory. He quotes Mitchell Waldrop (1992), who describes the edge of chaos as the one place where a complex system can be spontaneous, adaptive and alive – just the qualities we need if we are to survive. John Abbott (1996) also suggests that in complexity theory and chaos theory we may have the seeds of new possibilities. Commenting on the traditional curriculum currently enshrined in law, he comments:

> The idea of the curriculum divided into subjects, each approached in linear fashion so as to allow the supposed logical development of subject material, is a fundamental weakness of the National Curriculum. There is little regard for interconnectedness in contents, and none for the coherence of the whole curriculum taken together. In fact, the specialisation of the curriculum has been pushed further down the system into the primary schools in order, it appears, to remove Complexity. This is happening just at the time when research is revealing that long term learning and understanding depend upon the connections made in the mind between a diverse array of information and experience. In fact the brain seems more able to handle complexity than it does artificial simplicity.
>
> (Abbott 1996: 7)

Abbott further notes that in work outside education, greater emphasis is being placed upon holistic approaches to the study of systems – in business management, as well as in studies of environmental and ecological issues. He urges that education, too, must espouse these more systemic, integrated and holistic approaches to learning. In the twenty-first century, he stresses, '. . . education must prepare young people for a more confident participation in this more open, unpredictable understanding of natural phenomena' (p. 7).

Stephanie Pace Marshall (1996: 5) also thinks we need a new emphasis on these emerging insights. She suggests that these ideas can help us to:

- Create the empowered, entrepreneurial and relational learning communities we seek.
- Bring coherence, integration and simplicity to the complex systems in which we work.
- Build meaning, capacity and accountability into our enterprises.
- Bring all those committed to the education of children closer together as collaborators and partners in educational transformation.

But we must not rely only on external ideas and theories to help us out of the crisis. We have to look to our own capacities and creativity as well. The world of management is perhaps too awash with quick-fix approaches. What is needed is a new approach to renewal from within. Gareth Morgan (1993) emphasizes the central and crucial importance of a new deal for human imagination, and suggests that the challenges will be met not by adopting fancy panaceas or copying what other organizations seem to be doing, but by:

> ... engaging in some critical thinking for themselves, recognizing that they and their colleagues already have a vast treasure of insight and experience which they could and should be using. The challenge is to tap this insight and understanding in a constructive way.
>
> (Morgan 1993: 218)

We already have in the staffrooms of our primary schools all that we need to transform them. What we have to find is the time, opportunity, support, will and leadership to do it. What we can draw strength from, is that evolution is a process of constantly reaching out and beyond. The great innovations in primary education were pioneered by primary school teachers determined to discover better ways to help their children unfold their birthright, and they achieved this against a background of universal selection into grammar and secondary modern schools. Others have been inspired to follow, to unfold their own creativity in the complex environment of the primary school classroom.

CONCEPTS AND FRAMEWORKS

In transforming traditionally held assumptions about the processes of managing education in primary schools, we need to develop what Morgan (1988) describes as 'proactive mindsets', through which we increase our capacities to:

- look ahead;
- identify problems and opportunities;
- find ways of reframing problems so that negatives become potential positives, opening new avenues for development;
- grasp, shape and develop these opportunities so that they can be implemented.

Managers of the future, says Morgan, will have to develop their ability to *read* and anticipate environmental trends:

> They will need to develop antennae that help them to sense the critical issues and identify the emerging 'fractures' that will transform their organizations. At present these skills are largely intuitive

and the preserve of exceptionally astute individuals who have a
'good nose' for new developments. One important challenge will be
to find ways of developing these skills more explicitly.

(Morgan 1988: 4)

The agenda for conceptual development is a substantial one. The following six issues will certainly need to be near the top: change, error,
letting go, *ad hocracy*, time and thinking.

Change

Perhaps top of the list is the idea that significant change is possible.
Caroline Palmer (1994), in her exploration of the equitable company, suggests that two assumptions are so deep-rooted in the business world as
to have taken on the strength of incontrovertible truths. The first of these
is the belief that 'you cannot change human nature', and the second that
'you cannot run businesses that way'. To which her emphatic response
is, 'Oh yes you can'. If these assumptions were actually true, she argues,
we would still have slavery in this country and limited suffrage, and individuals would not have the human resources to overcome serious illnesses, bereavement and other serious life challenges. Leaders in primary
schools will be familiar with the cries of 'I'm too old to change' and
'That wouldn't work with my children'. Perhaps what such attitudes
reveal is a fear of change, of moving out of our comfort zones into the
unknown. Until we learn to see change as a journey of discovery, rather
than as a threat to our well-being, these fears will continue.

Error

Second on the agenda comes a new approach to failure. The very word
has the categoric ring of disaster about it. We are all familiar with the
phrase 'learning from our mistakes', but few of us will have encountered
its more positive partner, 'learning from our successes'. Fear of failure
and avoidance of mistake have become two of the most pernicious constraints on human creativity. In attempting to transform our preoccupation with the avoidance of mistakes, Charles Handy (1994) suggests that
we need to be more imaginative in our understanding. He suggests an
important distinction between two types of error:

Type 1 getting it wrong
Type 2 not getting it right, or as right as it could have been

For far too many of us, success is avoiding as many Type 1 errors as
possible. We do not like being wrong for we have grown up to believe

that getting things right is what makes us worthy. We also fail to attend seriously enough to Type 2 errors. These are often errors of omission, rather than commission. In schools, a good deal of learning failure is caused by punishing Type 1 errors, and in not encouraging enough Type 2 errors to provide sufficient experience to learn from. In the future, we will need to accept the improbability of getting anything right first time. We must learn to see that the actions we undertake in the pursuit of desirable goals are stages on the journey to success, full of meaning and possibility. Engines have governors to correct them when they speed up. We regard such a feedback measure as sensible and creative, but we do not think of the engine as having made a mistake. The key question is not 'What has gone wrong and who is to blame?', but 'What actually happened and what can we do now?'.

Writing about improvement-focused organizations, Tom Peters (1988) urges us not only to develop a more robust tolerance of faults, failures, errors and mistakes, but positively to accept them and encourage dialogue about them. One way to change fear of failure into acceptance of the inevitable, he argues, is to put it on the agenda:

> Talk it up. Laugh it up. Go around the table at a project group meeting or staff meeting: Start with your own most interesting foul up. Then have everyone follow suit. What mistakes did you make this week? What were the most interesting ones? How can we help you make more mistakes, faster?
>
> (Peters 1988: 261)

If we really do learn from our mistakes, then we need to keep making them in order to keep learning.

Letting go

Letting go is not easy. In gentler times, when we could afford long lead-in times to development projects, we took pains to anticipate likely difficulties and plan for them. The complexity of the modern world defies this cautiousness. When getting into action quickly, we must be alert to incidents and events, and take corrective action where necessary. This will mean stopping things that don't seem to be working and ditching those things that have not fulfilled their expectations. These may include management systems, new procedures, policy initiatives and, from time to time, the abandonment of whole projects. In the search for the new and the successful, we must try things out, and then not be afraid to jettison them if they do not work as well as we hoped. In particular, 'We must be prepared to let go of old perceptions, old attitudes, old ways of seeing things and take on the new with a freshness, vitality and freedom it demands of us' (Evans and Russell 1990: 13).

Ad hocracy

Creative extemporization will be one of the characteristic features of those schools determined to rise out of the current difficulties and dilemmas. They will exude a new spirit of curiosity, enquiry and imagination in their striving to succeed. Alvin Toffler (1971), in *Future Shock*, his classic examination of the effects of fast change on our lives, noted that such a spirit is not compatible with traditional structures, particularly bureaucratic ones, and that as we witness their breakdown we will witness the arrival of 'a new organizational system that will increasingly challenge, and ultimately supplant bureaucracy. This is the organization of the future. I call it "Ad hocracy"' (p. 120).

The structures we create, particularly management ones, will need to be less permanent and more temporary than ever before. Staff will participate in small teams, cross-disciplinary partnerships and short-term strategic alliances in order to introduce the constant short-term improvements that will characterize change in the future.

Time

One of the greatest causes of frustration and stress in organizations today is the perception that there is not enough time. This is a conceptual trap. Time itself remains unchanged in the sense that it carries on in the same way as it has for millions of years. We need to see that it is circumstances that are different, and that our increased workloads have overwhelmed us before we have been able to take stock of them.

This obsession with time management is perhaps temporary, as we adjust our attitudes and our metabolism to a more frantic pace of living and working. The secret lies not in finding smart ways to do more and more, but in how we manage the relationship between what we have to do and the time available to do it in.

Small and occasional additions to role requirements can usually be assimilated, but what we have witnessed is a significant role change. The difficulty lies in the fact that this role modification is one of increase, not adjustment – teachers' roles have not been redefined, they have simply been expanded. Effective workload management requires the balance of work required to time available to be maintained. For this to be achieved, some tasks and responsibilities have to be dropped or reallocated as new ones arise.

Most of us have grown up in a society more concerned with completion than with effort. From an early age we are driven to hurry up, to get things finished, to be in bed on time and never to be late. Punctuality has become an obsession, and many of us have a dread about appearing tardy or too casual about times and deadlines. Some of us would rather be an hour early than a minute late. Phrases such as 'Get your skates on!', 'Knuckle down!', 'Apply yourself!' and 'Get your act together!' can haunt us with their insistence on gaining the approval of others, whatever the costs.

Socialization has also placed great emphasis on perfection, that second best is simply not good enough. We sometimes shy away from starting a task because we do not have enough time available to achieve the standards we believe are required. Often our procrastination is to do with a lack of confidence to do it well enough.

While lack of time seems to be the problem, time is, in fact, one of the key resources for realizing our ambitions. One of the first challenges to improved effectiveness is seeing time as a resource rather than as a difficulty, an opportunity rather than a problem. Instead of asking how we should manage our time, we should be asking what it is we want to achieve. The first step towards more effective time management is to decide what we want to get out of life, not what we think we have to do.

One way of helping us to change our concepts of time is to recognize that while we do have a great deal to do, we don't have to do it all at once. We need to develop the capacity to place each task and project in the queue for our attention. Also, we need to develop a very capacious backburner where we can put things as they await our attention. While it is never easy to say 'No' to people, we can develop the knack of giving them a realistic target date which reflects current plans and priorities. If this doesn't satisfy those who make the demands on us, then they must assist us to increase our resources. Double the staff of a primary school and it will do most things by return of post.

We need to see that time, like money, is a finite resource – there is only so much of it available. Few members of staff are prepared to fund major school developments from their own financial resources, yet they seem quite prepared to cancel their personal lives to fund the time required to carry out professional tasks. Time must come from the same concept of a budget that we apply to financial management. When we plan a project, not only must we allocate a financial budget, we must provide a time budget too. This will involve us in determining the sort of outcome and result we can hope to achieve within time budget limits. Time is provided at a cost. At present the costs to personal well-being, health and social welfare are too high. There is a major task for senior managers here, to operate time budgets with the same diligence they apply to their financial ones. Just as we accept that significant financial overspends cause problems, we have to accept that time overspends also do.

Thinking

One of the most astonishing features of most work organizations in this country is the contempt extended to those who stop to think. It is not that thinking is wrong but that we must not be seen to be doing it, because it looks as if we are doing nothing. Try sitting down for a quiet think in any busy organization and within moments someone will be enquiring if we are all right. It never occurs to them that we might be thinking up the organization's next big idea or solving its knottiest problem. Working hard means being seen to be doing something. We need to find a new place for quiet thinking, professional contemplation and reflection, since the challenges ahead will demand ingenuity, imagination and the very best our mental faculties can produce.

Many of us will remember the exhortations to think harder when we were at school, but will also recall that nobody ever taught us to do it in the first place. Thinking is something we demand, but never teach about. The journey into the future will require three distinct types of thinking: critical thinking, reflective thinking and visual thinking. Each will serve distinct but important purposes.

Critical thinking is more hard-edged, involving the intellect. Stephen Brookfield (1987: ix) describes it thus:

> When we become critical thinkers we develop an awareness of the assumptions under which we, and others, think and act. We learn to pay attention to the context in which our actions and ideas are generated. We become sceptical of quick fix solutions, of single answers to problems, and of claims to universal truth. We also become open to alternative ways of looking at, and behaving in, the world.

This sort of thinking will be needed as we work to build new principles and practices in our management of learning in schools:

> When we think critically, we come to our judgements, choices and decisions for ourselves, instead of letting others do this on our behalf. We refuse to relinquish the responsibility for making the choices that determine our individual and collective futures to those who presume to know what is in our own best interests. We become actively engaged in creating our personal and social worlds. In short we take the reality of democracy seriously.
>
> (Brookfield 1987: x)

Brookfield suggests that there are four principal aspects to critical thinking:

1 *Identifying and challenging assumptions.* Testing the taken-for-granted nature of assumptions and generalizations against our own experiences and understanding. Questioning and challenging passively accepted traditions and habitual patterns.

2 *Challenging the importance of context.* Developing awareness of the

importance of relating our thinking to the context in which it is set. Practices, structures and actions are never context-free.

3 *Imagining and exploring alternatives.* Thinking beyond the obvious and the immediately logical. Adopting different perspectives and standpoints. Thinking laterally and imaginatively.

4 *Developing reflective scepticism.* Being wary of claims to universal truth or ultimate explanations. Because others think differently than we do, does not mean that they are right.

It will become increasingly important to back our own judgements and work from our own unique experience and contexts. Not only do we need to develop our own thinking skills, we need to make sure that the children we teach develop theirs and are helped to understand more of its intricate possibilities than we ever were.

Reflective thinking involves standing back and exploring our experience for meaning and significance. It is the means by which we learn deliberately from our experience so that we can make choices to continue and repeat those parts of our experience which bring fulfilment and success, and seek ways to change those which bring dissatisfaction and frustration. The process of review described in Chapter 6 involves this sort of thinking, and we will need to employ it in our individual capacities as well. Appraisal is one procedure which deliberately engages us in reflection, scanning recent experience for successes and difficulties, but is so infrequent as to be an event rather than a constant process. What we will need in the future are daily opportunities to stand back, to take stock and to examine the dynamics of our work and its many implications. Sharing our thinking with others increases our capacity to make sense of complexity and a good deal of staff development time will need to be allocated to reflective dialogue.

Visual thinking involves using the more spatially oriented right hemisphere of the brain, rather than the more literal and logically oriented left hemisphere. Traditional patterns of teaching have employed a virtually exclusive left brain approach, and many of us have entered adult life with our capacities for visual thinking seriously under-developed. As well as seeking literal definitions for professional ideas, we also need to engage in visualizing what they will look like in practice. One of the causes of fear of change is that we cannot imagine what the outcome will be. We need to harness the enormous power of our visual imagination, and employ it in our planning for the future, both in terms of developing visions of the sort of school we want and in relation to shorter-term projects and tasks.

Such an agenda has significant implications for professional development, and we will need to expand considerably the traditional horizons of professional development to encompass the conceptual challenges ahead.

TRANSFORMING THE CURRICULUM

As we move inexorably closer to a new century and a new millennium, it is important to consider the framework for learning that both the children and the adults of the future will need. While our traditional framework of subjects provided security drawn from long experience, it is dangerous to assume that what seemed useful in the past will necessarily serve the changing needs of the future. In their study of schools for the twenty-first century, Per Dalin and Val Rust (1996: 145–6) consider this issue of curriculum design:

> It will become increasingly difficult to define a comprehensive curriculum, both because the knowledge revolution will bring new and important knowledge into the school arena, and because the students' needs will constantly be changing. In all likelihood educational officials will likely move away from detailed teaching plans and focus more on general and thematic goals. They will attempt to define what is fundamental and exemplary.

The task of detailed curriculum design, they suggest, will again become the responsibility of educators working together within their schools. It will involve the identification of those areas where detailed knowledge and deep understanding will become increasingly important as the next century unfolds. Whatever happens, we need to accept the need for continuous modification and change. The essence of the curriculum will be its temporary focus, and its adaptability to new circumstances and situations. We will need to resist the temptation for a big reform movement that will attempt, once again, to write the curriculum in stone.

However, it will be unwise to discard all that we have learnt about subject disciplines and cross-curricular dimensions until we are clear that a more useful and manageable framework has emerged. We certainly need imagination and debate. What is required is a new synthesis of the factors which have traditionally been separated and kept apart – what we learn, how we learn it, how it is taught, who teaches it and how we will be able to use it. The National Curriculum is a subject-specific and content-based framework for education in schools. It ignores issues of teaching and learning, and the future uses to which the knowledge acquired through it might profitably be used. It is time to bring these powerfully related factors into a new synthesis. We need to appreciate the inevitable connectedness of all the parts. This can be illustrated as shown in Fig. 9.2.

At the heart of this framework is the learning process – what actually happens when learners and teachers work together to achieve understanding and proficiency. Three very distinct but powerfully connected factors feed into this process: the curriculum itself, the learners for whom

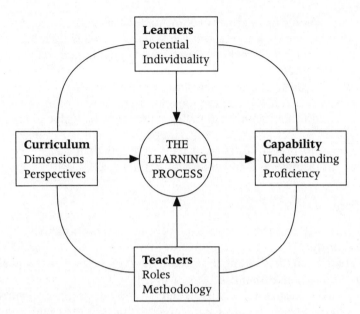

Figure 9.2   A framework for education in schools.

it is devised, and the teachers who strive to bring it to life. The outcome is not a set canon of knowledge, but a whole variety of understandings and proficiencies which provide a rich resource for the management of human life on the planet. This framework does not claim to be the model which we should adopt, but is offered as a model to stimulate thinking and discussion.

The learning process

While we have one of the most detailed content specifications for our professional work in schools, we have one of the least documented explanations of the learning process. Much of our pedagogy is a collection of rules of thumb handed down over the generations. We have no professional council which can provide descriptions of good practice, and the business of trying to make any sense of the enormous complexities of learning and teaching are left to academics who publish their ideas, and to the practitioners who get on as best they can. As Chapter 4 has suggested, we have significantly underestimated the intricate and complex nature of teaching, traditionally viewing it from an instrumental and mechanistic perspective as imparting known information to passive pupils in lecture halls and classrooms. Any departure from this tradition tends to be labelled 'progressivism' and dismissed as pernicious dogma.

Primary schools have always taken the learning process seriously and much of what we do know about the ways to manage learning in classrooms has been developed by imaginative practitioners supported by insights and understandings from academic research. School development plans need to focus on learning much more than on curriculum, for this is where much necessary development needs to take place. Few schools, amidst their plethora of policy statements, have documents about the learning process, and yet what happens moment by moment in the classrooms of our schools is far more important than elegant classifications of knowledge and targets for attainment.

Curriculum

The traditional subject curriculum is undoubtedly adaptable, having existed for thousands of years. It is not that such a way of organizing the content for learning is wrong, but that it may not be sufficiently pliable to accommodate the demands of the future. It is a sign of rigidity that we have tended to respond to changing demands by devising cross-curricular themes like citizenship education, careers education, sex education and environmental education. This puts the subject taxonomy under enormous pressure, since it is often difficult to find ways of organizing two distinct approaches to content – subject learning and thematic learning.

In primary schools, we have seen a variety of modes used. The Schools Council project 'Aims into Practice in the Primary School' (Ashton *et al.* 1975) proposed a model consisting of six areas for personal development: intellectual, physical, aesthetic, spiritual/religious, emotional/personal and social/moral. In 1985, the Department of Education and Science published *The Curriculum from 5–16*, which emphasized five important curriculum issues: breadth, balance, relevance, differentiation and progression. This was an important move towards placing the management of learning at the heart of curriculum design and development, but the initiative was short-lived, and three years later the rigidly subject-based curriculum for all age groups became part of government policy.

What would happen if we took a completely fresh look at the way we organize the interconnected phenomena affecting our lives and then used this as a basis for curriculum design? In his study of new and emerging paradigms in areas such as science, technology, sociology, information technology, political and economic science and management theory, Alvin Toffler (1980) proposed a new classification, based on six interconnected dimensions or spheres. This ground plan of human activity and experience, he claimed, brought together significant areas for particular consideration but also emphasized the dynamic nature of the connections and relationships within spheres and between spheres. In simplified form, Toffler's model can be summarized as:

- *Technosphere*: energy systems, production of goods and services, distribution systems.
- *Sociosphere*: social institutions and organizations, social behaviour, social trends.
- *Infosphere*: communication systems, information technology, mass media.
- *Biosphere*: ecology, climate, medical science.
- *Powersphere*: political systems, power and authority, human rights.
- *Psychosphere*: human identity and experience, personal behaviour, relationships.

This is only one example of how human activity, both in personal experience and in the wider world, can be classified. Such models and classifications can help us into new territories of thinking and speculating, as we struggle to find more effective ways to define the curriculum. There are numerous other starting points for curriculum design and development and our professional think tanks will need to be busy in the years ahead if we are to find relevant, flexible and imaginative ways of conceiving the content of learning for our schools.

Learners and teachers

We need to bring to our considerations of learning much greater attention to the participants in the whole process. It is the pupils who will take over the world when their time comes, and they need to be involved in the means by which they are prepared for that awesome responsibility. Not one official document has been produced explaining the National Curriculum to the children for whom it was designed. This gives some indication of the low expectations of understanding held about our pupils, and a measure of the disregard held for their own hopes and aspirations.

There is also the vital question of how we define, describe and explain the processes of teaching. Like the learning process with which it interacts, teaching is regarded in a mechanistic way. A great deal of work needs to be done if we are to understand more fully the complexities of the relationship between teacher and taught and to produce more comprehensive and detailed explanations of good practice.

The continuing development of information technologies will enable children to undertake for themselves at home, through CD Rom and allied technologies, a good deal of the basic work currently done by schools. Within the first decade or so of the next century, this will present schools with a fundamental question about the role of schools in what John Abbott (1996) describes as 'the learning society'. The law insists that our children receive an appropriate education, not that they attend school.

It is likely that we will see a fragmenting of full-time attendance in schools and a greater incidence of part-time contracts, where children use local schools for those parts of their learning they cannot do better for themselves. This, rather than competition for full-time places, currently the panacea for improving standards, will bring real market forces into the schooling system. Patterns of teaching will have to change to accommodate these shifting patterns. We need to attend to our own professional methodologies and practices quickly before events force us into crisis action.

Not only do we need to review quite radically the programmes of training through which teachers qualify. More time needs to be devoted to pedagogical issues in teacher training programmes and a greater focus on the management and leadership skills outlined in this book. Some teacher education institutions are recognizing the need to send young teachers out into schools able and prepared to help pupils understand the complexity of the world they are growing up in. A range of teacher education initiatives are described in *Developing the Global Teacher* (Steiner 1996), many of which concern preparing teachers to help pupils learn effectively about the complex dynamics of the present world, and how to develop their teaching approaches as the world continues to change. A key theme of this study is the notion of global citizenship with all its personal, social and political implications. We are no longer educating for a particular national imperative. The children in our primary schools now will live their lives in the next century, and some may even survive it. The business of teaching is badly in need of redefinition.

Capability

The goals our society currently sets for its learners are subject-specific and tied to detailed objectives which can be measured on a ten-point scale. Such is our ambition for the children in our schools. It is interesting to see how other countries express their educational ambitions. In 1994, the Norwegian Department of Education produced a new curriculum framework (Dalin and Rust 1996). Among its declarations are a set of six goals for schooling:

1 A person searching for meaning.
2 A creative person.
3 A working person.
4 An enlightened person.
5 A cooperating person.
6 An environmentally friendly person.

What a stunning contrast between this and our own statements of intent. What is interesting is that statements like this adorn the brochures produced by many primary schools for parents. Such an approach to learning is central to their philosophy of education and schooling, but sadly it has been held up to ridicule and contempt.

In specifying the planned outcomes from the learning process, we need to look beyond that which can be simply measured. The model outlined in Fig. 9.2 suggests three aspects to the outcomes of learning. First, we need to think in terms of capability, rather than knowing. Knowledge is highly desirable and vital to our survival and well-being, but it is incomplete. Education needs to produce people capable of acting in their own and the world's best interests. Two states of being become vital to this: understanding and proficiency. Schools have been instructed to concentrate on knowledge and skill performance. Capability goes well beyond this, envisaging the practical uses to which understanding and proficiency will need to be put. Such an enhanced view of learning enables us to help pupils to prepare for an active and creative role in the world. It recognizes that learning is for living, not just for knowing, and it helps us to build the life-centred curriculum that our future citizens so desperately need.

In their study of children's visions of the future, David Hicks and Catherine Holden (1995: 77–8) noted that by the end of their primary school years, children are increasingly aware of the complexity of social, economic and environmental issues in the world around them:

> They are concerned about their own future and that of their local community and are fairly optimistic that the quality of life will improve for the majority. They are less optimistic about the global situation improving . . . Between the ages of 7 and 11 children's ideas about the environment and global issues develop a great deal but this is not generally as a result of the taught curriculum. Pupils indicate that they have had little teaching in this area and would welcome more. They wish to be better informed about the world around them and better able to contribute to its future.

This raises the whole question about the role of the curriculum in helping children to prepare for the future. In his work on The Global Futures Project, David Hicks (1994a: 12–13) has emphasized the importance of this futures dimension in children's learning and offers a nine-point rationale:

1 *Pupil motivation.* Pupil expectation about the future can affect behaviour in the present; for example, that something is, or is not, worth working for. Clear images of desired personal goals can help stimulate motivation and achievement.

2 *Anticipating change.* Anticipatory skills and flexibility of mind are important in times of rapid change. Such skills enable pupils to

deal more effectively with uncertainty and to initiate, rather than merely respond to, change.

3 *Critical thinking.* In weighing up information, considering trends and imagining alternatives, pupils will need to exercise reflective and critical thinking. This is often triggered by realizing the contradictions between how the world is now and how one would like it to be.

4 *Clarifying values.* All images of the future are underpinned by differing value assumptions about human nature and society. In a democratic society, pupils need to be able to begin to identify such value judgements before they can themselves make appropriate choices between alternatives.

5 *Decision-making.* Becoming more aware of trends and events which are likely to influence one's future, and investigating the possible consequences of one's actions on others in the future, leads to more thoughtful decision-making in the present.

6 *Creative imagination.* One faculty that can contribute to, and which is particularly enhanced by, designing alternative futures is that of the creative imagination. Both this and critical thinking are needed to envision a range of preferable futures from the personal to the global.

7 *A better world.* It is important in a democratic society that young people develop their sense of vision particularly in relation to more just and sustainable futures. Such forward-looking thinking is an essential ingredient in both the preserving and improving of society.

8 *Responsible citizenship.* Critical participation in democratic life leads to the development of political skills and thus more active and responsible citizenship. Future generations are then more likely to benefit, rather than lose, from decisions made today.

9 *Stewardship.* Understanding the long- and short-term consequences of current local and global trends, as well as the action needed to change these, can lead to a sense of stewardship both for the planet now and in the future.

In his wise and inspiring examination of the struggles and complexities of being a teacher, Robin Richardson (1990) emphasizes the need for radical thinking about the future direction of education and calls for a new synthesis between two important traditions that have tended to be separated in the debate about educational development. The first of these is the learner-centred tradition, essentially humanistic and optimistic. This needs to embrace a concern for equality, creating a powerful new educational purpose for our work in the years ahead.

The second tradition is concerned with building equality, and with resisting the trend for education merely to reflect and replicate inequalities in wider society of race, gender and class; it is broadly pessimistic in its assumptions that inequalities are the norm wherever and whenever they are not consciously and strenuously resisted. Both traditions are concerned with wholeness and holistic thinking, but neither, arguably, is complete without the other. There cannot be wholeness in individuals independently of strenuous attempts to heal rifts and contradictions in wider society and in the education system. Conversely, political struggle to create wholeness in society – that is equality and justice in dealings and relationships between social classes, between countries, between ethnic groups, between women and men – is doomed to no more than partial success and hollow victories, at best, if it is not accompanied by, and if it does not in its turn strengthen and sustain, the search for wholeness and integration in individuals.

(Richardson 1990: 7)

This echoes Southworth's call for our schools to develop models of authority which reflect both these important traditions, so that our children will have early and active opportunities to learn through, and within, both.

The future has a variety of calls upon us and there is much important work to be done. Given the support from neighbourhood, community and the nation as a whole, primary schools are well placed to meet these demanding challenges and to make the new breakthroughs in practice and process that are so urgently needed.

◆10◆ NEW MILLENNIUM EDUCATORS

This book has raised a challenging agenda for those who will take primary school education into the next millennium. As the paradigm shift accelerates, new people will emerge with fresh ideas, new skills and qualities, and new visions of what is possible. Many of whom David Hicks (1994b) describes as 'new utopians' are already working in the system, striving to make our primary schools the nourishing foundation for a more humanistic, equal and optimistic world. Emerging from a variety of perspectives is a view of what these new millennium educators will be like. All of us will have some of the qualities that characterize them, but no-one is likely to have them all.

Towards the end of his long life working with people on the edge of change, Carl Rogers (1980) wrote of the qualities of those he described as 'emerging persons'. Finding them in all walks of life, he noted their determination to rise above orthodoxy and convention in the pursuit of what they really believe in. What unites them, he observed, was the fact that they present a new face to the world, a pattern which has not been seen before, except perhaps in rare individuals. He highlighted eight qualities in particular, and these are listed in Table 10.1.

Another view of the transformative person is provided by Marilyn Ferguson (1982), who, in her classic study of the emerging paradigm shift, noted a cluster of factors continually mentioned by the numerous people who were the subjects of her research:

- *Awakening*: a new quality of attention in life, as if seeing things for the first time and experiencing a new sense of awe and wonder.
- *Self*: realizing that our lives have a mission and that we have the capacity and drive to reach beyond traditionally imposed limitations.
- *Process*: a realization that how we do things is often more important than what we do, that learning is more important than information and that caring is more important than keeping. The journey is the

Table 10.1 Qualities of emerging persons

- *Authenticity*: a deep concern to communicate the truth of themselves without deceit, dissembling or concealment
- *Care*: a genuine desire to be of help to others, sharing themselves and their time in a gentle and non-do-gooding way
- *Community*: a capacity to build close and intimate working relationships in groups, committees and teams
- *Humanistic*: a distrust of only scientific solutions to human affairs, and a powerful regard for the possibilities of human potential
- *Inner world*: a concern for their own self-awareness, of searching for their own patterns of thought and feeling in order to take more responsibility for themselves
- *Ecology*: a commitment to the natural environment and to the care of species; a concern for sustainable rather than exploitative lifestyles
- *Change*: an awareness of the constancy of change in the world and an adventurous approach to their own development
- *Self-trust*: a trust in their own experience, and a distrust of external authority in that it claims to know what is best for them

---

destination: 'When you enjoy the trip, life is more fluid, less segmented; time is more circular and subtle'.

- *Body/mind*: the reconnection of parts of ourselves that have become separated. Our mind is part of the same self as our body, brain is not always better than brawn, dancing is not less worthy than thinking.
- *Freedom*: we can operate beyond apparent restrictions and inhibitions. We can disengage from the *cultural trance*, which makes us obedient to the behaviours that others have designed for us, because they are best for them.
- *Uncertainty*: an appreciation that curiosity is a vital driving force in life, that a sense of awe and mystery is what makes our lives interesting and purposeful. We become more interested in the magnitude of the questions than the certainty of the answers.
- *Intuition*: rediscovering what has been marginalized as merely a feminine trait – a sort of whole-brain knowing based on hunches, urges and gut reactions.
- *Vocation*: a sense of direction in our lives that is greater than a goal, making our way in life towards something, of realizing we are doing what we really want to do with our lives.
- *Responsibility*: an attitude to our life and work that goes beyond duty and guilt – the act of giving back or responding, combined with the realization that we can make a difference in the world and that our contributions are significant to the wider scheme of things.
- *Choice*: realizing that we are in charge of our own destinies in more

senses than we had originally thought; what we think, believe, hope for, who we like and dislike and what our aspirations and ambitions are.

- *Support*: the realization that although we may sometimes feel lonely, we are not alone, but part of a significant trend towards new types of friendship, partnerships, alliances, networks and communities.
- *Beyond fear*: fear does not have to be our prison – fear of self, fear of others, fear of loss, fear of embarrassment, fear of being fooled. Realizing that a fear of looking foolish is transformed by the sudden recognition that *not* changing, *not* exploring, is a far more real and frightening possibility.

The psychologist and writer Sam Keen (1991: 126) notes a set of qualities in the people he describes as pathfinders: 'In every society, there are extraordinary men and women who, for a variety of reasons, stand outside the social consensus, shatter the norms, and challenge the *status quo*'. The qualities he identifies as especially significant are: exploration, courage, a sense of wonder, self-awareness, and fun and joy.

1. *Exploration*. Explorers, Keen suggests, need to know how to be lost comfortably, and he quotes from the journals of the Danish philosopher Soren Kierkegaard:

And this is the simple truth: that to live is to feel oneself lost. He who accepts it, has already begun to find himself, to be on firm ground. Instinctively, as do the shipwrecked, he will look round for something on which to cling. And the tragic, ruthless glance, absolutely sincere because it is a question of his salvation, will cause him to bring order into the chaos of his life. These are the only genuine ideas, the ideas of the shipwrecked. All the rest is rhetoric, posturing, farce.

(Keen 1991: 134)

2. *Courage*. Keen points to psychological courage which, he suggests, is rarer than its physical counterpart. He observes that those of us who have not dared to wrestle with anxiety, fear, hate, anger, pride, greed, longing, grief, loneliness, despair, impotence and ambivalence, may find ourselves bowing obediently to authority and established opinion and never claiming the territory of our own psyches for ourselves. Too many of us, he suggests, succumb to infantile guilt and shame, which alienates us from our true self, and prevents us from looking at experience from our own personal viewpoints.

Inevitably, when we are young we interpret our lives through the eyes of parents, adults and authorities. We are little and they are big. We automatically adopt their values, their religion and their philosophy of life. Our conscience is their conscience. But at some point, we must kick Dad and Mother, priest, pope and president out of our psyche and seize the authority for our own lives. We must become responsible for our own values and visions . . . Growing in the fullness of our humanity means that we become co-authors of the rules by which we will agree to have our lives judged.

(Keen 1991: 144–5)

3. *A sense of wonder.* The notion of personal awakening involves climbing out of the illusory trap which has been woven around us since birth, and finding a new sense of wonder about the possibilities in our own lives. Keen quotes Dag Hammarskjold (1964), a former Secretary General of The United Nations:

We die on the day when our lives cease to be illumined by the steady radiance, renewed daily, of a wonder, the source of which is beyond all reason.

(Keen 1991: 156)

Self awakening involves taking hold of purpose and mission and approaching life with a restless searching and questing.

4. *Self-awareness.* Working to increase our self-awareness creates the possibility of more choices in our lives, and gives us a more self-directed relationship with the external world. We are more able to work for the common good because we are more in touch with the good in ourselves, and with the power we have to influence and change things.

5. *Fun and joy.* The final quality Keen refers to is the capacity of these newly emerging persons to have fun. This is not to say that they don't take life seriously, but they really enjoy doing so. Somewhere in the past, the idea was developed that serious endeavour and fun are incompatible, that we will never be successful if we treat life frivolously. Keen notes this lack of joy in our society, and the energy we seem to invest in avoiding any sense of enjoyment or conviviality.

In his book *The Reinvention of Work*, Matthew Fox (1994) notes that if there is no bliss in our work, no passion, no ecstasy, then we have not yet found our work. We have not experienced that sense of awakening that sets pathfinders on their way. We may have a job, but we do not have work, the vocation referred to by Marilyn Ferguson. In describing the many pleasures of his own work, Fox (1994: 96) observes:

I also experience joy and delight in my work as a teacher. I love watching students grow and watching them watching themselves growing . . . I love students who teach me things – maybe the questions they ask or questions they resolve or experiences they share or arguments they put forward . . . I love to watch what students do with their learning, say one, two, or five years after they leave my classroom. It gives me a sense of history and of taking part in the ongoing stream of wisdom flowing into future generations.

Tom Peters (1994) talks of how in our organizations we conspire to force people to lead hopelessly dull lives in a thoroughly undull world. A school leaver once remarked sadly, that her school had not helped her to appreciate just how wonderful the world is. Charles Handy (1994) notes a worker in Dresden, who after the changes in working patterns following German reunification, observed that it may have been a bad system, but there was a lot of time and energy for family, friends, festivals and fun, whereas now it all seems to be about profit, performance, pay and productivity.

The final perspective on post-millenium educators comes from Judi Marshall (1994). She makes a distinction between traditional, male-focused qualities, and emerging female-focused values which western societies in particular have selectively neglected, but which are now re-emerging in the lives of both men and women. Her analysis of these values and qualities links closely with the ideas of newly emerging people described above, and with the shifting paradigm in human affairs with which the whole of this book has been concerned.

Marshall stresses that her analysis is not about distinction and the qualities demonstrated separately by men and women. In emphasizing the necessary partnership between men and women implicit in the paradigm shift, she likens the different qualities to the yin and yang in Taoist philosophy – the essentially opposite, but complementary, forces that characterize existence. The two sets of qualities are set out in Table 10.2.

In emphasizing this disposition, Marshall makes a number of key points. First, that both men and women have access to both sets of qualities. As a result of social roles, biological make-up and socialization, women are more likely to resonate with the female principles and men with the male ones. Secondly, that both sets of principles can take either an adaptive or a degenerative form. Control, for example, can be appropriately employed but can also be used destructively; and openness can involve putting yourself at a disadvantage if used inappropriately. Thirdly, that while both sets of qualities are potentially equal and complementary, patriarchal societies have given preference and special significance to the male values, while often minimizing and belittling the female ones. Marshall (1994: 168) summarizes her viewpoint thus:

> There are qualities to which our culture has limited access, because they have been systematically suppressed. Early Equal Opportunities initiatives did little to change this relative valuing because they urged equality for the ways women are the same as men. Now some women and men are realizing that our suppressed heritage is still

Table 10.2 Complementary human values

Male values	Female values
Self-assertion	Affiliation
Separation	Attachment
Control	Receptivity/merging acceptance
Competition	Cooperation
Focused perception and clarity	Awareness of patterns, wholes, contexts
Rationality	Intuition
Analysis	Emotional tone
Discrimination	Synthesis
Activity	Being
Reaching out	Grounding/holding
Thrusting	Containing
Underlying themes	
Independence	Interdependence
Focus	Openness
Control of the external world	Cycles of change and renewal
Questing outward	Looking within

largely untapped, and that public world values are often distorted as they are male values pursued in isolation.

For educators in primary schools there is important work to be done. As we move towards and into the twenty-first century, this work will determine whether or not the traditions of primary education have been sustained during the recent struggles for its soul. Those who work in primary schools must reassert these traditions and move them forward for new times and changed circumstances. A second great wave of primary school innovation is needed to move schooling out of the tight and confined corner it has been forced into, a wave of change that will once again provide for the youngest children in our schooling system, a beginning to their formal education which honours their birthright and offers new hope to their own cherished visions for the future.

The unfolding of potential is the challenge for each of us. If we are to help the pupils we work with to feel a full sense of their own awesome potential for learning and growth, we need to be as authentic as we can in our own communications with them. We have inherited shameful beliefs in the propriety of misleading children, of deflecting their questions and inhibiting their curiosity.

We must resist the obsession with appearance and performance and ensure that our children find in their schools some time and space for the inner life too, time and space to search for the patterns of their own thoughts and feelings. If we are to develop in them a powerful sense of vocation and a vision of what is possible, we will need to cherish their fears as well as their dreams.

There is important work to be done in redeeming professional integrity and regaining a proper pride in our service to young children. We must reclaim some of our lost authority as educators. The traditions of primary education are worthy and honourable, and it is only through a sure sense of what we believe in for our children that we can create the schools that are worthy of them.

We sometimes ask our young relations what they want to be when they grow up. The answer is often short or non-commital. Some years ago the following story appeared in a network newsletter:

> An elderly relative enquired of a child – what do you want to be when you grow up? The child replied – When I grow up, I want to be a painter, a poet, a prophet, a priest, a watchmaker, a lover, a shepherd, a swineherd, a mechanic, a miller, a brewer, a baker, a cobbler, a farrier, a rock singer, a mother, a father, a weaver, a nurse, a helper, a friend, a sailor, a dancer, an architect, a woodcutter, a quarrier, a bricklayer, a carpenter, a plasterer, a plumber, a philosopher, a survivor, a teacher, an explorer, a cook, a television presenter, a stowaway, a climber, a traveller, a finder, a storyteller, a clown, a potter, a stranger, a forester, a gardener, a river, a mountain, a distant cry, a shower, a full moon, a reason. That's what I want to be.

Which primary school did this child attend, one wonders, and what sort of careers education was offered? For those who work in primary schools, this story touches on their dreams. It even, perhaps, contains the beginning of a bold new attainment target.

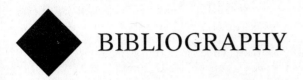

BIBLIOGRAPHY

Abbott, J. (1996) Chaos and complexity: Or just education? In *Education 2000 News*, March 1996. Letchworth: Education 2000.

Anthony, P. (1994) *Managing Culture*. Buckingham: Open University Press.

Argyris, C. (1960) *Integrating the Individual and the Organization*. New York: John Wiley.

Argyris, C. (1982) *Reasoning, Learning and Action: Individual and Organizational*. San Francisco, CA: Jossey-Bass.

Ashton, P., Kneen, P. and Davies, F. (1975) *Aims into Practice in the Primary School*. London: Hodder and Stoughton.

Ashton-Warner, S. (1980) *Teacher*. London: Virago.

Barth, R. (1988) School: A community of leaders. In Lieberman, A. (ed.), *Building a Professional Culture in Schools*. Columbia: Teachers College Press.

Bellman, G. (1990) *The Consultant's Calling*. San Francisco, CA: Jossey-Bass.

Bennis, W. (1989) *Becoming a Leader*. London: Hutchinson Business Books.

Bly, J. (1990) *Iron John*. Shaftesbury: Element.

Bohm, D. (1980) *Wholeness and the Implicate Order*. London: Routledge and Kegan Paul.

Brookfield, S. (1987) *Developing Critical Thinkers*. Buckingham: Open University Press.

Canfield, J. and Wells, H. (1976) *100 Ways to Enhance Self-concept in the Classroom*. Englewood Cliffs, NJ: Prentice-Hall.

Capra, F. (1983) *The Turning Point*. London: Flamingo.

Clegg, A. (1980) *About Our Schools*. Oxford: Blackwell.

Dalin, P. and Rust, V. (1996) *Towards Schooling for the Twenty-First Century*. London: Cassell.

Department of Education and Science (1985) *The Curriculum from 5–16: Curriculum Matters 2*. London: HMSO.

Dickens, C. (1961) *Hard Times*. London: Collins.

Donaldson, M. (1978) *Children's Minds*. London: Fontana.

Egan, G. (1977) *You and Me*. Belmont, CA: Brooks/Cole.

Evans, R. and Russell, P. (1990) *The Creative Manager*. London: Unwin.

Ferguson, M. (1982) *The Aquarian Conspiracy*. London: Granada.

Fox, M. (1994) *The Reinvention of Work*. San Francisco, CA: Harper.

Fullan, M. and Hargreaves, A. (1992) *What's Worth Fighting for in Your School?* Buckingham: Open University Press.

Gardner, H. (1993) *Multiple Intelligences.* New York: Basic Books.

Garratt, B. (1987) *The Learning Organization.* London: Fontana/Collins.

Hall, E. and Hall, C. (1988) *Human Relations in Education.* London: Routledge.

Handy, C. (1976) *Understanding Organizations.* London: Penguin.

Handy, C. (1989) *The Age of Unreason.* London: Business Books.

Handy, C. (1994) *The Empty Raincoat.* London: Hutchinson.

Herzberg, F. (1966) *Work and the Nature of Man.* New York: Staple Press.

Hicks, D. (1994a) *Educating for the Future: A Practical Classroom Guide.* Godalming: World Wide Fund for Nature.

Hicks, D. (1994b) *Preparing for the Future: Notes and Queries for Concerned Educators.* London: Adamantine Press.

Hicks, D. and Holden, C. (1995) *Visions of the Future: Why We Need to Teach for Tomorrow.* London: Trentham Books.

Hoffer, E. (1985) In O'Toole, J. (ed.), *Vanguard Management.* New York: Doubleday.

Howe, D. (1993) *On Being a Client: Understanding the Processes of Counselling and Psychotherapy.* London: Sage.

Jeffers, S. (1992) *Dare to Connect.* London: Piatkus.

Jung, C. (1971) *Psychological Types.* Princeton, NJ: Princeton University Press.

Keen, S. (1991) *Fire in the Belly.* New York: Bantam.

Kelly, K. (1994) *Out of Control: The New Biology of Machines.* London: Fourth Estate.

Kinsman, F. (1990) *Millennium: Towards Tomorrow's Society.* London: W.H. Allen.

Krok, R. (1977) *Grinding it Out: The Making of McDonalds.* New York: Berkley.

Kuhn, T. (1970) *The Structure of Scientific Revolutions.* Chicago, IL: University of Chicago Press.

Lewin, K. (1936) *Principles of Topological Psychology.* New York: McGraw-Hill.

Marshall, J. (1994) Re-visioning organizations by developing female values. In Boot, J., Lawrence, J. and Morris, J. (eds), *Managing the Unknown by Creating New Futures.* London: McGraw-Hill, p. 168.

Maslow, A. (1954, 1970) *Motivation & Personality.* New York: Harper and Row.

Maslow, A. (1978) *The Farther Reaches of Human Nature.* London: Penguin.

McGregor, D. (1960) *The Human Side of Enterprise.* New York: McGraw-Hill.

Mezzirow, J. (1983) A critical theory of adult learning and education. In Tight, M. (ed.), *Adult Learning in Education.* London: Croom Helm.

Mintzberg, H. (1973) *The Nature of Managerial Work.* New York: Harper and Row.

Morgan, G. (1988) *Riding the Waves of Change: Developing Managerial Competencies for a Turbulent World.* San Francisco, CA: Jossey-Bass.

Morgan, G. (1989) *Creative Organization Theory.* Newbury Park, CA: Sage.

Morgan, G. (1993) *Imaginization: The Art of Creative Management.* London: Sage.

Mulligan, J. (1988) *The Personal Management Handbook.* London: Sphere.

Murgatroyd, S. (1988) Consulting as counselling: The theory and practice of structural consulting. In Gray, H. (ed.), *Management Consultancy in Schools.* London: Cassell, pp. 66–78.

Oaklander, V. (1978) *Windows to Our Children.* Moab, UT: Real People Press.

Orr, D. (1992) *Ecological Literacy: Education and Transition to a Postmodern World.* Albany, NY: State University of New York Press.

Pace Marshall, S. (1996) The vision, meaning and language of education transformation. In *Education 2000 News*, March 1996. Letchworth: Education 2000.

Palmer, C. (1994) The equitable company. In Boot, J., Lawrence, J. and Morris, J. (eds), *Managing the Unknown by Creating New Futures*. London: McGraw-Hill, pp. 59–77.

Peck, M.S. (1985) *The Road Less Travelled*. London: Rider.

Peters, T. (1988) *Thriving on Chaos*. London: Macmillan.

Peters, T. (1992) *Liberation Management*. London: Macmillan.

Peters, T. (1994) *The Tom Peters Seminar*. London: Macmillan.

Peters, T. and Waterman, R. (1982) *In Search of Excellence*. New York: Harper and Row.

Phares, J. (1976) *Locus of Control in Personality*. NJ: General Learning Press.

Postman, N. and Weingartner, C. (1971) *Teaching as a Subversive Activity*. London: Penguin.

Prigogine, I. (1979) *From Being to Becoming*. San Francisco, CA: W.H. Freeman.

Richardson, R. (1990) *Daring to be a Teacher*. Stoke-on-Trent: Trentham Books.

Rogers, C. (1980) *A Way of Being*. Boston, MA: Houghton Mifflin.

Rosenblatt, D. (1975) *Opening Doors*. New York: Harper and Row.

Roszak, T. (1981) *Person/Planet*. London: Granada.

Rotter, J.R. (1966) Generalized expectancies for internal versus external control of reinforcement. *American Psychologist, 26*.

Rowan, J. (1983) *The Reality Game*. London: Routledge and Kegan Paul.

Rowan, J. (1992) *Breakthroughs and Integration in Psychotherapy*. London: Whurr Publishers.

Senge, P. (1990) *The Fifth Discipline*. London: Century Business.

Smail, D. (1987) *Taking Care*. London: J.M. Dent.

Southworth, G. (1995) *Looking into Primary Headship*. London: Falmer Press.

Steiner, M. (ed.) (1996) *Developing the Global Teacher: Theory and Practice in Initial Teacher Education*. Stoke-on-Trent: Trentham Books.

Szent-Gyoergyi, A. (1974) Drive in living matter to perfect itself. *Synthesis*, Spring.

Taylor, F. (1947) *Scientific Management*. New York: Harper and Row.

Toffler, A. (1971) *Future Shock*. London: Pan.

Toffler, A. (1980) *The Third Wave*. London: Pan.

Waldrop, M. (1992) *Complexity*. New York: Simon and Schuster.

Webb, R. and Vulliamy, G. (1996) *Roles and Responsibilities in the Primary School*. Buckingham: Open University Press.

Whitaker, P. (1983) *The Primary Head*. London: Heinemann Educational.

Whitaker, P. (1993a) *Managing Change in Schools*. Buckingham: Open University Press.

Whitaker, P. (1995) *Managing to Learn*. London: Cassell.

Whitmore, D. (1986) *Psychosynthesis in Education*. Wellingborough: Turnstone Press.

Zinker, J. (1977) *Creative Processes in Gestalt Therapy*. New York: Vintage Books.

INDEX

Abbott, J., 146, 147
accountability, 85–6
achievements, 95–9
ad hocracy, 112, 115, 150
affection, 116
ambiguity, 6–7
ambition, 43–5
appearance, 16–17
attainment target, 168

Barth, R., 131
Bellman, G., 138
Bennis, W., 66
Brookfield, S., 152

Canfield, J., 80
capability, 158–61
Capra, F., 47
careers education, 168
change, 148
  aspirational, 29
  conceptual, 25–7
  emotional, 28–9
  practical, 29–30
chaos, 2
classroom life, 78–86
climate and ethos, 40–1
cohesion, 45–8
collaboration, 110–12
community, 48–50
competition, 125
complexity, 3, 5–6, 10, 50, 87
confusion, 3, 9

control, 116, 144, 166
cooperation, 84–5
creativity, 54, 160
curriculum, 4, 6, 8, 9, 38, 42, 43,
  154–61
curriculum coordination, 132–4

Dalin, P., 154, 158
decision-making, 83–4
development projects, 99–107
Dickens, C., 24
differentiation, 38
diversity, 40

Egan, G., 76–7
error, 148–9
essence, 16–17
evaluation, 96–9
Evans, R., 149
everyday life, 92–5
evidence, 97
evolutionary challenge, 143–7
evolutionary crisis, 1, 12

federal management, 94–5
Ferguson, M., 162, 165
flexibility, 41–2, 109
force/field analysis, 102–3
Fox, M., 165
functional staffing, 93

Gardner, H., 56–7
Garratt, B., 15, 30

gender, 56, 166
getting organized, 123

Hall, C., 52
Hall, E., 52
Hammarskjold, D., 165
Handy, C., 2, 3, 8, 13, 78, 146, 148, 166
Hicks, D., 27, 159, 162
hierarchies, 20, 114, 125, 144
Holden, C., 27, 159
holistic, 46–7, 146
hopes and intentions, 88–92
Howe, D., 138, 140
human potential, 44, 51, 74, 75, 138–41
humanistic education, 52

inclusion, 115–16
individualism, 110–12, 125
inheritance factor, 23–5
integration, 45–8, 146
intensity, 36–40
interactions, 123–4
interpersonal world, 136–41

Jeffers, S., 139
job descriptions, 134–6
judgement, 97

Keen, S., 164, 165
Kierkeggard, S., 164
Kinsman, F., 67
Krok, R., 108
Kuhn, T., 18

leadership
   catalytic, 141
   concepts, 127–30
   life focused, 129, 145
   modes, 136
learning organization, 30–3, 110
learning process, 154–6
letting go, 149
Lewin, K., 102–3
life centred learning, 51, 54–8
locus of control, 83

management structures, 20–1, 124–6
managerial skills, 60–1
Marshall, J., 166
Maslow, A., 139
mental models, 32
Mintzberg, H., 11, 63
Morgan, G., 140, 143, 147, 148
Mulligan, J., 81–2
multiple intelligences, 56–7
Murgatroyd, S., 99–100

National Curriculum, 5, 8, 16, 17, 23, 24, 35, 36, 40, 46, 55, 154
nostalgia, 13–16

observation, 96–7
Ofsted (Office for Standards in Education), 5, 23, 98
operational modes, 62–4
optimism, 43–5
organic management, 93–4
organizational cultures
   dimensions, 72
   forces, 72
   issues, 77–8
   nutrients, 75–7
   syntropic/entropic, 72–4, 94
   toxins, 74–5
   transactions, 71
   zones, 70–1
organizational dynamics, 19
organizational forms, 42–3, 114–15
organizational vision, 91–2
organizational world, 34–6
Orr, D., 51
outcomes, 95–9

Pace Marshall, S., 146
Palmer, C., 148
panic, 13–16
Peck, M.S., 10
people dynamics, 21–3
personal mastery, 31
personhood, 55–6
Peters, T., 2, 13, 18, 27, 90, 137, 149, 166

Phares, J.E., 83
planning, 82, 88–105
post-modernism, 8, 45–7
Postman, N., 57
pressure, 4, 109
project organization, 114

responsibility
  to school, 118
  to self, 116–17
  to team, 117–18
review, 105–7, 124
Richardson, R., 160
richness, 36–40
Rogers, C., 130, 162
role definitions, 134–6
Roszak, T., 53, 66
Rotter, J.R., 83
Rowan, J., 138, 139, 144, 145
Russell, P., 149
Rust, V., 154, 158

self-managed learning, 98
Senge, P., 30, 32, 33, 89, 142
Simon, E., 89–90
skilful simultaneity, 41
Southworth, G., 134, 142, 161
spontaneity, 37–8
Steiner, M., 158
stress, 12–13, 28, 29
subtlety, 39
systems thinking, 31

task, 122–3
task-focused management, 112–14
teaching as leadership, 64–7, 130–4
teaching skills, 58–62
team
  building, 122–4
  leadership, 130–4
  learning, 33
  membership, 15–18
  option, 109–10
thinking, 151–2
  critical, 152–3, 160
  reflective, 153
  visual, 153
time, 150
Toffler, A., 2, 13, 58, 150, 156
turbulence, 11

uncertainty, 8–9
unpredictability, 39

vision, 32, 90–2
Vulliamy, G., 6, 132

Waldrop, M., 146
Webb, R., 132
Weingartner, C., 57
Wells, H., 80
Whitmore, D., 53, 65
workload management, 150

Zinker, J., 53, 54

ROLES AND RESPONSIBILITIES IN THE PRIMARY SCHOOL
CHANGING DEMANDS, CHANGING PRACTICES

Rosemary Webb and Graham Vulliamy

- How are teachers planning and implementing the National Curriculum at Key Stage 2?
- How have the recent policy and legislative changes affected the roles and responsibilities of class teachers, curriculum co-ordinators, deputy headteachers and headteachers?
- How are primary schools managing the current plethora of innovations and what can be learned from their experience?

Based on qualitative research in 50 schools throughout England and Wales, this book portrays teachers' work as it is currently experienced in the post-ERA context of multiple innovations. It examines the impact of the National Curriculum and assessment on classroom practice, curriculum organization and planning at Key Stage 2. Drawing on the wealth of ideas and successful practices shared with the authors by the teachers in the study, it demonstrates how classteachers, curriculum coordinators, deputy headteachers and headteachers are tackling the new demands of their expanding roles. An analysis of the management of change reveals a growing tension between collegial and top-down directive managerial styles, which is fundamentally affecting the culture of primary schools. Through presenting what is actually happening in primary schools in contrast to prescribed educational orthodoxies, this book makes a vital contribution to the debate on the future of primary education.

Contents
Introduction and methodology – The changing context of primary education – Changing demands on classroom practice – Changing curriculum organization and planning – The changing role of the curriculum coordinator – The changing role of the deputy headteacher – The changing role of the headteacher – Managing whole school change in the post-ERA primary school – References – Index.

192pp   0 335 19472 9   (Paperback)   0 335 19473 7   (Hardback)

MENTORING AND DEVELOPING PRACTICE IN PRIMARY SCHOOLS
SUPPORTING STUDENT TEACHER LEARNING IN SCHOOLS

Anne Edwards and Jill Collison

Is school-based initial teacher training just another burden to be imposed on primary school teachers or is it an exciting new development which could be the key to the development of primary education?

This book will be of interest to anyone who wants student teachers to make the most of their time in primary schools. Its central theme is that students learn best when supported by *active mentors*. Active mentors are learning teachers who are able to develop as professionals in the schools in which they work. These schools may in turn have much to gain from closer relationships with higher education. Throughout the book primary education is described as a community of practice to which all primary education specialists, wherever they are based, have contributions to make. The book is designed as a key text for modular staff development programmes in either schools or universities. Evidence from classroom mentoring is provided as starting points for the development of mentor practices through action research. In addition each chapter is followed by suggestions for further reading and most end with ideas for professional development activities for mentors and their students.

The text pulls no punches on how demanding mentoring is but provides a wealth of advice on the development of students, mentors and ultimately of schools. It will be invaluable reading for mentors in schools and tutors in higher education institutions.

Contents
Section 1 – Frameworks and themes – Students as learners – Section 2 – Mentoring conversations – Mentoring in action in classrooms – Running seminars – Mentoring and subject knowledge – Pedagogy and initial teacher training – Mentoring and assessing – Section 3 – Mentors as researchers – Mentoring and school development – Making the most of relationships with higher education – Endpiece – References – Index.

192pp   0 335 19565 2   (Paperback)   0 335 19566 0   (Hardback)